CINDERELLA

A Pantomime

by Chris Denys and Chris Harris

JOSEF WEINBERGER PLAYS

LONDON

CINDERELLA
First published in 2001
by Josef Weinberger Ltd
12-14 Mortimer Street, London, W1T 3JJ

ISBN 0 85676 251 2

This Pantomime of **CINDERELLA** was first produced by the Bristol Old Vic Company at the Theatre Royal, Bristol on December 6th, 1995 with the following cast:

FAIRY CRYSTAL	April Walker
BARON HARDUP	John de Barham
INNKEEPER	Christopher Punter
GLADYS HARDUP	Mark Buffery
GERTRUDE HARDUP	Patrick Miller
BUTTONS	Chris Harris
CINDERELLA	Prue Clarke
PRINCE CHARMING	Penelope Woodman
DANDINI	Anna Rose
MAJORDOMO	Christopher Punter
VILLAGERS, TOYS, FAIRIES, LORDS and LADIES	The Dancers of ACRODANCE 2000

Directed by Chris Denys
Designed by John Elvery
Choreography by Gail Gordon
Music Directed by John O'Hara
Music Supervised by Neil Rhoden
Lighting Designed by Tim Streader
Sound Designed by Matt Valentine

Characters

FAIRY CRYSTAL

BARON HORATIO HARDUP

CINDERELLA as a Child

COUNTESS HARDUP II

THE HON MS GLADYS HARDUP

THE HON MS GERTRUDE HARDUP

CINDERELLA

INNKEEPER

BUTTONS

HRH PRINCE CHARMING

DANDINI

MAJORDOMO

HUNTSMEN *and* WOMEN

VILLAGERS

TOYS, DOLLS, TEDDY BEARS

CINDERELLA DOUBLE

BUTTONS DOUBLE

FAIRIES

FAIRY COACHMAN

FAIRY FOOTMEN

LORDS *and* LADIES

Scenes:

ACT ONE

PROLOGUE (*Before Panto Cloth*)

Scene One: THE VILLAGE GREEN – OUTSIDE HARDUP HALL
Scene Two: A STATEROOM IN THE ROYAL PALACE
Scene Three: THE FOREST IN WINTER
Scene Four: A COUNTRY LANE
Scene Five: TOYS 'R' BUTTONS (BUTTONS' SHOP)
Scene Six: HARDUP HALL – THE TRADESMAN'S
                  ENTRANCE
Scene Seven: LA BOUDOIR DE GLADYS ET GERTRUDE
                  HARDUP
Scene Eight: THE KITCHEN OF HARDUP HALL

Transformation to:

Scene Nine: THE FAIRY FOREST

ACT TWO

Scene One: THE BALLROOM OF THE ROYAL PALACE
Scene Two: IN THE DEPTHS OF THE FOREST – BY NIGHT
Scene Three: HARDUP HALL – THE TRADESMAN'S
                  ENTRANCE
Scene Four: THE KITCHEN OF HARDUP HALL
Scene Five: THE SAME COUNTRY LANE
Scene Six: THE BALLROOM OF THE ROYAL PALACE

AUTHOR'S NOTE

This Pantomime is intended to be "traditional" in that the Prince and Dandini are played by girls and Cinderella's awful sisters by men in hideous frocks, the story is told clearly with as much action and knock-about as possible and, very importantly, it is local to the town or city in which it is performed. It's also meant to be great fun – both for the audience and for those who perform and present it.

The local references in this script relate to Bristol – where it was first produced in 1995 so please feel free to localise as necessary and desirable.

Also, the staging is as described because we were working in beautifully equipped theatres with excellent design and production departments able to give us anything we asked for. It doesn't have to be like that, of course, and can be adapted to how much – or how little – you have at your disposal.

The stage directions, groundplans and indicated lighting, sound, follow-spot and pyrotechnic cues are only intended as suggestions and not to be in any way prescriptive.

The only sort of "flash" units allowed by Fire Officers these days are ruinously expensive and we always wrote our scripts with a liberal use of these effects only to cut them back to essentials when we saw what it was going to cost.

An optional "Slosh" scene is included at the end which, if you want it, is intended to follow on directly after the Trio (Act Two, Scene Three) as an extension of the scene.

The Music:
Pantomime audiences do like to know the tunes so we have always used either current and perennial favourites as written or taken well-known melodies and written lyrics which stand as part of the plot and move the story along.

Some of the music we have used is out of copyright (eg, the Act One Finale is set to a piece from *Princess Ida* and the Trio on page 61 is to Bizet's *L'Arlesianne* so these are clear) *but other melodies are still in copyright and you will need to pay for these if you use them through the Performing Rights Society* (who offer a special – and very reasonable – deal for Pantomimes).

Mostly, though, we have found that producers prefer to choose their own music to suit and show off the particular voices of their cast.

ACT ONE

Prologue – Before "Cameo" cloth. Music.

A Flash. (PyroQ.1; LXQ.1; FSQ.1) The FAIRY GODMOTHER appears resplendent DR. The characters appear in "cameos" behind the gauze (or Cameo Cloth) as she tells the story.

FAIRY: Long, long ago
                In a land I know,
                By a stream of crystal water,
                Lived Baron Hardup . . . *(LXQ.2) (The BARON appears.)*
                Of Hardup Hall
                And Ella – *(CINDERELLA, as a small child, appears and
                runs to embrace him.)* – his beautiful daughter.
                A widower, he,
                And motherless, she,
                Yet, together they were contented.
                'Til – most foolish of men –
                He married again . . .

                *(The STEPMOTHER appears between them, pushing them
                apart.)*

                He must have been demented.
                For the new wife came
                Like a hurricane
                And battered the pair apart.
                She'd a face that was good
                For chopping wood
                And a medal in marshal art.

                *(The STEPMOTHER fells the BARON with a karate chop
                and drives CINDERELLA away.)*

                But what was worse –
                As a further curse –
                She'd daughters of her own . . .

                *(The UGLY SISTERS appear from either side. One of them
                seizes the little ELLA, shakes her and pushes her off. They
                pose grotesquely.)*

                Who cast young Ella
                Down into the cellar
                To sleep on the stones alone.
                But, as the years flew,

The little girl grew
Into the fairest flower . . .

(The grown up CINDERELLA appears. The SISTERS are furious.)

And how the sisters
Booed and hissed her.
Her beauty made them glower!

(The STEPMOTHER produces a huge pie and tears at it with her teeth. She suddenly clutches her throat, chokes and falls over backwards out of sight.)

But then the bride
Overdid it and died
While guzzling in the larder.

(The UGLIES look down at her, shrug, and turn on CINDERELLA.)

But that didn't aid
The poor little maid –
Who was forced to work all the harder.
Now she must trudge
All day, and drudge,
And scrub and polish and sweep
And dust and scour –
Hour after hour –
And weep herself to sleep.

(A series of "freezes" of CINDERELLA working – the UGLIES being nasty during:)

FAIRY: The sisters drive her with spite and hate
While she cleans and scrubs from early 'til late
She lays the fires and cleans the grate
And does all that they tell her.
She must behave
As their humble slave.
And they call her . . .

UGLIES: CINDER-ELLA!!!

(Lights fade behind the Gauze.) **(LXQ.3)**

FAIRY: They cram and scoff
Like pigs at a trough

And then they yell for more.

UGLIES: *(Off)* MORE!!

FAIRY: They open accounts
             For enormous amounts
             At every department store.
             They spend on this and spend on that –
             On sequined gowns and silly hats –
             And the poor old Baron must pay the bills –
             For all their furbelows and frills –
             But, whatever they wear,
             The hideous pair
             Grow fouler and foustier yet
             And they think it a joke
             That the Baron is broke
             And up to his ears in debt.
             And so we meet him
             As the villagers greet him
             One bright December day –
             They've come – one and all –
             To Hardup Hall –
             To drive his cares away.

             (She exits as the Panto Cloth flies out **(FlyQ.1; LXQ.4;**
             FSQ.1A) *to reveal:)*

                          Scene One

The Village Green – outside Hardup Hall.

             Song: (OPENING CHORUS) HEY NEIGHBOUR
             (BARON, INNKEEPER and VILLAGERS)

INNKEEPER/   *(Trying to cheer up the BARON)* HEY, WHAT'S THE
POINT VILLAGERS: OF WORRYING,
             THOUGH YOU ARE STONY BROKE
             AND THE COUNCIL TAX IS THREE YEARS OVERDUE?
             WHEN THE BAILIFFS TAKE YOUR FURNITURE,
             JUST TREAT IT AS A JOKE,
             THERE ARE PEOPLE WHO ARE FAR WORSE OFF THAN
                                                       YOU!
             DON'T YOU SEE THE SUN IS SHINING ON THIS FINE AND
                                               FROSTY MORN?
             DON'T YOU HEAR THE ROBIN SING TO GREET THE DAY?
             BUT IT'S ALL A WASTE OF EFFORT IF YOU'RE MOODY
                                               AND FORLORN,

SO PAY ATTENTION WHEN WE SAY:

HEY, NEIGHBOUR! SAY, NEIGHBOUR!
HOW'S THE WORLD WITH YOU?
AREN'T YOU GLAD TO BE ALIVE THIS SUNNY
                           MORNING?
DID YOU NOTICE THAT THE SKY ABOVE IS BLUE?
THAT'S WHY WE SAY, NEIGHBOUR! HEY, NEIGHBOUR!
YOU KNOW WHAT TO DO –
SPREAD YOUR HAPPINESS AROUND YOU AS THE DAY
                           GOES BY,
YOU'LL FIND THE HABIT CATCHING IF YOU'LL ONLY·
                           TRY –
PUT A BIT OF LOVE AND LAUGHTER IN YOUR LABOUR –
HEY, NEIGHBOUR, THAT MEANS YOU!

BARON: What have I got to sing about? *(Holding up masses of paper.)* Look at this – bills, bills and more bills . . .

INNKEEPER: Oh, Baron I forgot to tell you. A man called while you were out.

BARON: Did he have a gigantic bill?

INNKEEPER: No. Just an ordinary nose.

BARON: I expect he wanted the Council Tax. But I can't pay it. I can't pay anything. What am I going to do?

INNKEEPER: You could sell some of that antique furniture. Why, some of it goes back to Louis the fourteenth.

BARON: Unless I keep up the payments, it *all* goes back to Louis on the fourteenth.

(FSQ.2)   *(CINDERELLA enters, carrying bucket and mop.)*

CINDERELLA: Hello, everybody . . .

ALL: Hello, Cinders . . .

BARON: Oh, poor Cinderella, you're not still slaving away, are you?

CINDERELLA: I've nearly finished, Daddy. Why, another nine hours and I can have a rest . . .

BARON: I won't stand for it any longer. I'm going to tell those terrible sisters of yours where to get off . . .

ALL: Oh no you're not!

BARON: *(Defiant)* Oh yes I am!

ALL: Oh no you're not!

BARON: *(Subsiding)* Oh no, I'm not . . .

INNKEEPER: You're just as scared of them as the rest of us.

CINDERELLA: But never mind them now . . . *(sings)*
              I HAVE DUSTED ALL THE FURNITURE
              AND POLISHED ALL THE FLOORS
              AND I'VE PUT A SHINE ON EV'RY POT AND PAN.
              I HAVE CHOPPED THE WOOD JUST LIKE I SHOULD
              AND DONE A SCORE OF CHORES
              AND IT'S ONLY FOURTEEN HOURS SINCE I BEGAN.
              I'VE PUSHED MY BROOM ROUND EV'RY ROOM
              AND NOW I'M NEARLY DONE
              ONCE I'VE TAKEN UP MY SISTERS' BREAKFAST TRAY –
              SO I'M SNATCHING JUST A MOMENT
              TO COME OUT INTO THE SUN
              AND TO GREET MY LOVELY FRIENDS AND SAY –

ALL: HEY, NEIGHBOUR! SAY, NEIGHBOUR!
              HOW'S THE WORLD WITH YOU?
              AREN'T YOU GLAD TO BE ALIVE THIS SUNNY
                                              MORNING?
              DID YOU NOTICE THAT THE SKY ABOVE IS BLUE?
              THAT'S WHY WE SAY, NEIGHBOUR! HEY, NEIGHBOUR!
              YOU KNOW WHAT TO DO –
              SPREAD YOUR HAPPINESS AROUND YOU AS THE DAY
                                              GOES BY,
              YOU'LL FIND THE HABIT CATCHING IF YOU'LL ONLY
                                              TRY –
              PUT A BIT OF LOVE AND LAUGHTER IN YOUR LABOUR –
              HEY, NEIGHBOUR, THAT MEANS YOU!

(FSQ.2A)

CINDERELLA: I must go . . . Gladys and Gertrude are off to the hunt and I
              have to clean their habits.

INNKEEPER: And they've got some very dirty habits.

UGLIES: *(Off)* CINDERELLA!!!!

BARON: Oh no! Look out!

INNKEEPER: It's the deadly duo.

BARON: It's Aliens Two . . .

CINDERELLA: I'd better go. It's . . .

(She runs one way and is confronted by GLADYS.)

CINDERELLA: Gladys!

(She runs the other way and bumps into GERTRUDE.)

CINDERELLA: Gertrude!

GLADYS: As usual! Loitering with these layabouts!

GERTRUDE: Hanging out with the hoi-poloi, you lazy little loafer, you!

GLADYS: Have you pressed my best dress?

CINDERELLA: Yes, Gladys.

GERTRUDE: And have you hironed my hunting habit?

CINDERELLA: Yes, Gertrude.

BARON: Hunting habit?

GLADYS: Of course. The Prince is going into the woods to hunt the wolf.

GERTRUDE: And we're going into the woods to hunt the Prince.

GLADYS: He comes of age this week . . .

GERTRUDE: So he'll have to get married . . .

GLADYS: And he's bound to ask me.

GERTRUDE: To do the catering?

GLADYS: You can scoff, Gerty, but I could marry anybody I please.

GERTRUDE: But you haven't pleased anybody yet.

BARON: But hunting? I didn't know you could ride.

GLADYS: Oh yes. *(Bending.)* I've got a wonderful seat.

(FSQ.3)

GERTRUDE: *(Kicking her)* And we've got such a wonderful day for it . . . *(Pushing villagers.)* Out of my way, you . . . pesky pongy pauperish peasants! Don't you know who I is? *(Sings.)* I'M THE BEAUTY QUEEN OF BEDMINSTER!

GLADYS: AND I'M MISS CANNON'S MARSH

GERTRUDE: WE ARE GIRLS WHAT WEARS OUR FORTUNES ON OUR FACE!

GLADYS: BUT I'M TWENTY AND UNMARRIED –

GERTRUDE: AND A SPINSTER'S LIFE IS HARSH

BOTH: SO WE'RE OFF TO HUNT A HUBBY IN THE CHASE!

GERTRUDE: NOT NO NAFF UNPLEASANT PEASANT!

GLADYS: NOT NO SWEATY SON OF TOIL!

BOTH: NOT NO BUMPKIN WHAT'S BEEN BRINGING IN THE HAY! NO!

GERTRUDE: THE MAN WE WANT IS CLASSY!

GLADYS: HE IS REGAL!

GERTRUDE: HE IS ROYAL!

BOTH: SO WHEN WE MEETS THE PRINCE WE'LL SAY:

ALL : HEY, NEIGHBOUR! SAY, NEIGHBOUR!
HOW'S THE WORLD WITH YOU?
AREN'T YOU GLAD TO BE ALIVE THIS SUNNY MORNING?
DID YOU NOTICE THAT THE SKY ABOVE IS BLUE?
THAT'S WHY WE SAY, NEIGHBOUR! HEY, NEIGHBOUR!
YOU KNOW WHAT TO DO –
SPREAD YOUR HAPPINESS AROUND YOU AS THE DAY GOES BY,
YOU'LL FIND THE HABIT CATCHING IF YOU'LL ONLY TRY –
PUT A BIT OF LOVE AND LAUGHTER IN YOUR LABOUR –

HEY, NEIGHBOUR, THAT MEANS YOU!

(FSQ.3A)

GLADYS: *(Shaking CINDERELLA)* Now, you! Get back into that castle and clean up our crops.

GERTRUDE: *(Shaking her)* And buff up our boots . . .

GLADYS: And pack us up a picnic . . .

GERTRUDE: And, while we're out hubbie-hunting, you'd better boil up our bathwater . . .

GLADYS: 'Cos us'll 'spect a super soapy soaking to soothe our saddlesoreness ce soir, see?

GERTRUDE: So, when you've done *everything* else . . .

GLADYS: . . . and left that kitchen *squeaky* clean . . .

GERTRUDE: You can forage in the forest for some fuel for the fire . . .

GLADYS: So don't just stand there.

BOTH: GO!! GO!! GO!!

(CINDERELLA runs off. BARON HARDUP is about to tiptoe after.)

GLADYS: *(Menacing)* And, Daddy!

BARON: *(Jumps)* Yes?

GLADYS: Find Buttons and send him to us at once.

GERTRUDE: Yes. We shall need him to soft-soap our saddles . . .

GLADYS: And grummet our girths . . .

BARON: Buttons? But he'll be busy in his toyshop – ever so busy – toys for the children – what with Christmas . . .

GLADYS: Toys for *children*?

GERTRUDE: Did you say . . . *children*?

GLADYS: *(To the AUDIENCE)* I *hate* . . . *children*!

GERTRUDE: Oh, I do so agree with you, Gladys! *Children!* Eaugh!!!
              Nasty, noisy, icky-sticky, loathsome little . . . NERDS!

GLADYS: We've a thousand and two jobs for Buttons to do. So go
              and find him – you, you and you!

GERTRUDE: Yes. Don't just stand there, you horrible lot.

BOTH: FIND BUTTONS!!!

              (They go.)

ALL: *(Running hither and yon, calling)* Buttons? Buttons . . .
              Buttons, where are you? BUTTONS . . . !!

(LXQ.5; FSQ.4)

              *(BUTTONS enters on an extravagant, four-wheeled (or
              three-wheeled – or even two-wheeled), pedal-contraption
              bedecked with whirling roundabouts, windmills, flags,
              streamers and hung all over with toys and teddies.)*

BUTTONS: Did somebody call? Hi, boys and girls, Mums and Dads –
              not forgetting the bus-pass brigade. I bet you can't guess
              what my name is.

AUDIENCE: Buttons.

BUTTONS: Somebody's been talking. Yes, it's Buttons. Cor, I'm worn
              to a frazzle, I tell you. I just never stop. It's go go go all
              the time. Baron Hardup's always on at me for a start. "Go
              on," he says, "Go off and get my season ticket for the
              Rovers." Then there's them ugly sisters . . . Have you seen
              them? Ugly? Even my pet pit bull, Cuddles, looks like
              Naomi Campbell next to them. And they never let up. It's
              "Buttons, do this!" and "Buttons, do that!" "Buttons,
              stand up!" "Buttons, sit down!" "Get me a burger! Get me
              a pastie!" I'll give 'em a pastie. Thing is, see, I haven't
              the time since I got me franchise – "Toys 'R' Buttons".
              Like the mobile shop? Stop me and buy one – when you
              hear me tinkle it's time for a teddy. Yes. I sell everything
              from teddies to trolls – from Mickey Mouse to Megadrives –
              from pogosticks to yo-yos! You name it – I've got it!
              Who said marshmallows? You've got me on a good day
              'cos I've got a marshmallow mountain – a glut – a overdose
              – so I'm allowed to give some away to my friends. But only
              if you help me. You see, I've got this problem . . . Wait for

it! I can't stop putting my hands in my pockets. If you see me putting my hands in my pockets, I want you all to shout out "Pockets!" Shall we have a little practice? That's very good. Now you can have your mallows and I can practice my forehand smash at the the same time. *(He bats marshmallows out into the auditorium – aided by the VILLAGERS, who throw them to him.)* But the trouble is . . . I do feel low.

AUDIENCE: Aaw . . .

BUTTONS: No, I feel lower than that. You see, I haven't seen Cinderella all day long and I do miss her. See, she's as busy as what I am so we do only meet at three for a cup of tea and comisserate with one another . . . Still, I mustn't get downhearted. I must always meet her with a smile because . . .

(LXQ.6)

Song: Whatever is the current Children's Favourite
(BUTTONS, VILLAGERS and AUDIENCE)

(Blackout.)   *(LXQ.7; FSQ.4A; FlyQ.2)*

(LXQ.8; SQ.1)

Scene Two

A Stateroom in the Royal Palace. We hear the screams of hundreds of girl fans off stage. PRINCE CHARMING enters in a fury, dressed for hunting, followed by DANDINI who carries a hunting horn.

DANDINI: But, Sire, there's a queue
Of girls waiting for you
Since six o'clock this morning.

PRINCE: Well, that's just tough –
'Cos I've had enough
Of their flattery and fawning.
They don't care for *me* –
It's my royalty –
That gets them so excited.
They don't come to view
Someone common like you.

DANDINI: Well, *I* might be delighted.

PRINCE:　　Aye, so you say.
　　　　　　But on show each day –
　　　　　　Like an animal in a zoo?
　　　　　　You'd very soon tire
　　　　　　Of "Your Highness . . . Oh, Sire . . ."
　　　　　　From that twittering wittering crew.
　　　　　　It isn't *me*
　　　　　　They want to see –
　　　　　　It's my crown that draws the crowd.
　　　　　　And every miss
　　　　　　Begging for my kiss . . .

DANDINI:　*I'll* kiss 'em – *I'm* not proud.

PRINCE:　　They don't give a damn
　　　　　　For me as I am.
　　　　　　It's my title that they're after.

DANDINI:　Hah!

PRINCE:　　But surely you see . . .

DANDINI:　Oh pardon me –
　　　　　　While I have a fit of laughter.

PRINCE:　　What?

DANDINI:　You make me sick!
　　　　　　You could take your pick.
　　　　　　You must be off your trolley
　　　　　　If I were you,
　　　　　　I'd grab a few.
　　　　　　You really are a wally.

PRINCE:　　*(Struck by the thought)* If *you* were *me*?

DANDINI:　Aye then you'd see.
　　　　　　I'd not waste time on cursin'

PRINCE:　　If *you* were *me* –
　　　　　　Then *I* could be –
　　　　　　An ordinary person.
　　　　　　Dandini, that's it!

DANDINI:　*(Uneasy)* Hang on a bit . . .

PPRINCE:　You've all the airs and graces
　　　　　　To fool the folk . . .

DANDINI: It was just a joke.

PRINCE: Oh no. We're changing places!

DANDINI: We'd never do it . . .

PRINCE: There's nothing to it.
                   You'll be the debs' delight.

DANDINI: *(Tempted)* D'you think I will?

PRINCE: It's utter brill –
                   They'll chase you day and night.

DANDINI: Alright, I'll swap.
                   Being poor's no cop.
                   I'll assume your princely duties.

PRINCE: Dandini will rule!

DANDINI: Hey, won't it be cool –
                   Surrounded by those beauties?

PRINCE: Dandini, you're on.
                   Let's see it done –
                   Before you change your mind. *(Taking off hat, sash, jewels, etc, and thrusting them at DANDINI.)*
                   Help me take off this
                   Badge of office.
                   It's yours, mate, I've resigned!

DANDINI: *Can* you do that . . . ?

PRINCE: Here, take my hat –
                   My sash, my sword, my cloak.
                   Now you alone
                   Are heir to the throne
                   And I'm an ordinary bloke.

DANDINI: *(Putting them on)* I must admit
                   They're a perfect fit.

PRINCE: You're a prince to the manner born.

DANDINI: *(Strutting)* Yaas! Now I shall go
                   To the hunt dontcher know.

Here fellow – *(Gives the PRINCE the hunting horn.)* – you
carry the horn!

(LXQ.9; FSQ.5)

Song: ON THE ROAD *(PRINCE and DANDINI)*

PRINCE: WHAT A GREAT IDEA!
                 NOW I CAN FIND A GIRL
                 WHO LOVES ME FOR MYSELF ALONE.

DANDINI: I FEAR IT'S CLEAR
                 THE PRINCE IS OFF HIS TREE
                 BUT WHAT A ROYAL PRINCE I'LL BE –
                 WHEN SEATED ON MY THRONE!

PRINCE: ARE YOU READY?

DANDINI: STRONG AND STEADY!

BOTH: OUR NEW LIFE HAS JUST BEGUN –
                 WHATEVER MAY BEFALL
                 WE'RE GOING TO HAVE A BALL
                 AND A BASINFUL OF FUN!

                 WE'RE ON THE ROAD TO ANYWHERE –
                 WITH NEVER A HEARTACHE AND NEVER A CARE.
                 COMRADES BOTH – BEST OF FRIENDS –
                 READY FOR ANYTHING THE GOOD LORD SENDS.
                 ON THE ROAD TO ANYWHERE
                 WHERE EV'RY MILESTONE SEEMS TO SAY
                 THAT, THROUGH ALL THE WEAR AND TEAR,
                 THE ROAD TO ANYWHERE
                 WILL LEAD TO SOMEWHERE SOME DAY –
                 WILL LEAD TO SOMEWHERE SOME DAY!

DANDINI: Now where are these beauties?
                 These cuddlesome cuties?
                 I'm not a one for shyness.
                 I'll make 'em pay.
                 You! Lead the way.

PRINCE: *(Bowing low)* No. After you, Your Highness!

                 (Blackout.)   *(LXQ.10; FSQ.5A; FlyQ.3)*

(LXQ.11; FSQ.6)

Scene Three

The Forest in Winter.

Song: HUNTING SONG *(To the tune of Galloping Major)*
(BARON, MAJORDOMO, HUNTSMEN and WOMEN)

ALL: ROLLICKING THROUGH THE FOREST,
WE'RE THE UPPER-CRUST CREME DE LA CREME.
WE'RE THE PRIDE OF THE COUNTY, BY GOSH!
SO WELL-DRESSED AND SO FRIGHTFULLY POSH!
WE GALLOPED AROUND 'TIL WE LAWST ALL THE
                                HOUNDS
SO WE SEARCHED EV'RY DINGLE AND DELL
BUT, IN BRACKEN AND BOGS,
THERE'S NO SIGN OF THE DOGS –
NOW WE'VE LAWST ALL THE HORSES AS WELL!
SO IT'S ON SHANKS'S PONY WE GO!
'COS WE'RE HUNTIN' THE WOLF DONTCHER KNOW?

AND –
WE'RE –

HOT ON THE TRAIL
THROUGH THE SNOW AND THE HAIL
WE DON'T GIVE A DAMN FOR THE WEATHER.
THROUGH TEMPEST AND FLOOD,
THOUGH WE'RE COVERED IN MUD,
WE'RE FROLLICKING OVER THE HEATHER!
A 'HUNTIN' WE WILL GO!
FLATTENING ALL BEFORE US –
HEY! HEY! CLEAR THE WAY!
HERE COMES THE TALLYHO CHORUS!

BARON: ALL THE BEST PEOPLE ARE HERE!

MAJORDOMO: FOR THEY'VE NOTHING AT ALL ELSE TO DO!

BARON: WHEN THE WOLF HEARS US SHOUT:

ALL: VIEW HALLOO!

BARON: HE STAYS HOME FOR THE DAY –

MAJORDOMO: WOULDN'T YOU?

BOTH: WE GO CRASHING ABOUT
                 AND WE CHORTLE AND SHOUT
                 WE NEVER KILLED ANYTHING YET.
                 BUT IT'S EVER SUCH FUN
                 WHEN IT'S OVER AND DONE
                 AND WE GO LIMPING HOME TO THE VET.

BARON: SO, IF YOU'VE GOT A LIKING FOR PORT –

MAJORDOMO: TAKE UP HUNTING, IT'S JOLLY GOOD SPORT!

ALL: SO –
                 WE'RE –

                 HOT ON THE TRAIL
                 THROUGH THE SNOW AND THE HAIL.
                 WE DON'T GIVE A DAMN FOR THE WEATHER.
                 THROUGH TEMPEST AND FLOOD,
                 THOUGH WE'RE COVERED IN MUD,
                 WE'RE FROLLICKING OVER THE HEATHER!
                 A'HUNTIN' WE WILL GO!
                 FLATTENING ALL BEFORE US –
                 HEY! HEY! CLEAR THE WAY!
                 HERE COMES THE TALLYHO CHORUS!

                 (As they exit, a wolf howls in the distance. (SQ.2;
                 LXQ.12; FSQ.6A) CINDERELLA enters through the trees.)

CINDERELLA: Oh dear. I wish they hadn't all galloped off like that –
                 leaving me alone. That wolf is a terrible menace and I don't
                 mind admitting I'm frightened . . . *(She begins to gather
                 sticks.)*

                 (There is a deep throaty sound "reebee".)

CINDERELLA: What was that? Could that be the wolf? It seems to be
                 coming from . . .

                 *(She creeps towards a fallen log. A FROG (puppet) pops
                 up.)*

FROG: REEBEE.

CINDERELLA: Oh! It's only a silly old frog . . .

                 (The FROG does a double take.)

CINDERELLA: I'm sorry. I didn't mean to call you silly or old. I was just
                 so relieved you weren't the wolf.

FROG: 'S alright.

CINDERELLA: You can talk!

FROG: Oh yerse . . .

CINDERELLA: You're a bit hoarse.

FROG: Got a person in my throat.

CINDERELLA: You want your neck to be tickled?

FROG: MMMMM.

CINDERELLA: *(Tickling)* Do you like that?

FROG: MMMMM.

CINDERELLA: Where do you live? In the Royal lake?

FROG: No. Fishponds.

CINDERELLA: You're not a *magic* frog, are you?   The sort you find in
               fairy stories who grant three wishes?

FROG: Try me.

CINDERELLA: Three wishes?   That's easy. First, I wish that Daddy could
               get all his money back.

FROG: Abracadabra . . . Wheee!

CINDERELLA: Second, I wish my sisters weren't always so cross with me.

FROG: Izzy wizzy let's get busy. Wheee! Er . . . One . . . Two . . .
               and three?

CINDERELLA: Third . . . *(Shyly)* I wish I could meet a handsome prince . . .

FROG: *(Bowing)* Ta-daaah!

CINDERELLA: You're not a prince.

               *(The FROG leans forward, puckered up, making kissing
               noises.)*

CINDERELLA: You mean if I kiss you, you'll turn into a prince?

FROG: *(Nodding vigorously)* Mmmmm.

CINDERELLA: Alright. You're a very nice frog anyway. We'll see what happens . . .

             (She kisses the FROG. He shudders with ecstasy and keels over and BUTTONS falls out from behind the log with the frog puppet.)

CINDERELLA: Oh, Buttons, it was you all the time. How could you lead me on like that? I should have known better. There's no such thing as magic.

BUTTONS: *(Shocked)* OH! May you be forgiven! You mustn't ever say that. Of course there is such a thing as magic.

CINDERELLA: No there isn't.

BUTTONS: Oh yes there is.

CINDERELLA: Oh no there isn't.

BUTTONS: *(Leading the AUDIENCE)* Oh yes there is! But only if you believe. You have to believe, Cinders. You just don't believe enough.

             (She turns away from him.)

BUTTONS: I'm sorry, Cinders. Please don't be cross with me. You know I'd do anything for you . . . anything.

CINDERELLA: I'm sorry too, Buttons, you're always so good to me . . . But I'd better get on and gather the wood – or Gladys and Gertrude will go mad . . .

BUTTONS: Pair of fat old pheasants!

CINDERELLA: You mean peasants. A pheasant is a funny old bird that grows wild in the woods.

BUTTONS: That's them.

CINDERELLA: There's something coming . . . Could it be the wolf?

             (FAIRY CRYSTAL (as a very old lady) hobbles through the woods.)

BUTTONS: No. Just a pensioner looking for her bus pass . . . Got to
                dash. The Baron sent me to dress his horse for the hunt.

CINDERELLA: Dress his horse?

BUTTONS: *(Going)* It's a clothes horse. *(As he exits he puts his hands
                in his pockets.)*

AUDIENCE: Pockets!

BUTTONS: Just testing! *(Exits.)*

                *(The OLD LADY falters and is about to fall when
                CINDERELLA rushes to save her.)*

CINDERELLA: *(Helping her to sit on the log)* Why you poor old lady.
                Are you ill?

FAIRY: Not ill, my dear. Just old and feeble. I came to gather
                sticks to make a fire to drive the cold from my ancient bones
                but I fear it's rather too much for me these days . . .

CINDERELLA: Here. Take mine. I can easily gather more.

FAIRY: Oh no, Cinderella. If your sisters come home and find no
                fire in the grate, they'll beat you.

CINDERELLA: I can gather more and be home before them if I run . . . But
                how do you know about my sisters? And how did you
                know my name?

FAIRY: I know a great many things. The past – the present – and
                the future.

CINDERELLA: The future?

FAIRY: *Your* future . . . I know, for instance, that you will start to
                gather more sticks – but that something will stop you.

CINDERELLA: Something bad?

FAIRY: Oh no. Something wonderful.

CINDERELLA: But . . . Who *are* you?

FAIRY: Just an old woman – wandering in the woods. And now I
                must go, my dear.

CINDERELLA: Let me carry the sticks for you . . .

FAIRY: Thank you, no. You have already shown me kindness enough.

CINDERELLA: But at least I could see you home . . . Where do you live?

FAIRY: Wherever *you* are.

CINDERELLA: Wherever *I* am? I really don't understand . . .

FAIRY: Perhaps it is best – for now – that you don't . . .

CINDERELLA: Please let me help you . . .

FAIRY: No. You must stay here. This is the place.

CINDERELLA: What place?

FAIRY: For you, a very magic place. You will return to this glade often in the years to come – to remember . . .

CINDERELLA: To remember . . . ?

FAIRY: . . . that it was on this very spot – on this very day that you met . . . your own true love . . .

CINDERELLA: *(Looking around)* My own true love?

(There is a Flash (LXQ.13; PyroQ.2) and the FAIRY disappears.)

CINDERELLA: I . . . Why, she's gone . . . vanished . . . Was she really here? Was I dreaming? Why no. I gave her the wood I'd gathered. And now I must gather more and hurry home or I'll be in for it. *(She begins to gather sticks among the trees.)*

(SQ.3)

(DANDINI and the PRINCE enter, breathless.)

DANDINI: We've left them far behind, your Highness . . .

PRINCE: Who?

DANDINI: I mean, Dandini . . .

PRINCE: They'll soon catch up. Then you'll see what it's like to have awful people fawning over you.

DANDINI: They're not all awful, surely.

PRINCE: Just you wait and see. I never meet anybody who isn't gross and hideous and vile and . . . *(He turns and finds himself face to face with CINDERELLA – he gasps.)* . . . the most beautiful girl I ever saw in my life . . .

(Music.) (LXQ.14; FSQ.7)

CINDERELLA: Oh . . . ! *(She drops the sticks.)*

PRINCE: *(Helping her to gather them)* Here, let me help you. *(They bang their heads.)* Oh, I'm so sorry . . .

CINDERELLA: It doesn't matter. It was my fault.

PRINCE: No it was mine . . . *(Sings.)* FAIREST OF ALL THE FAIR –
OH, PRINCESS OF THE FOREST –
BRIGHTER THAN ANY STAR –
PRAY TELL ME WHO YOU ARE . . .

CINDERELLA: NO-ONE, SIR –
JUST A SERVANT WHO GOES ABOUT HER DUTY
(Aside.) HE'S SO HANDSOME . . .

PRINCE: *(Aside)* SUCH A BEAUTY . . .

BOTH: WHAT ENCHANTMENT BRINGS WE TWO TOGETHER
FROM AFAR?

PRINCE: BE MY OWN!

CINDERELLA: YOURS ALONE!

PRINCE: BY ALL THE STARS ABOVE ME,

CINDERELLA: CAN THIS BE TRUE?

PRINCE: I LOVE YOU!

CINDERELLA: I LOVE YOU!

BOTH: I LOVE YOU!

(LXQ.15; FSQ.7A; SQ.4)

CINDERELLA: But no . . . I don't even know you. I . . . Forgive me. I must
go . . .

PRINCE: Go? But why?

CINDERELLA: I must . . . I have work to do. I'm only a servant.

PRINCE: That's alright. I'm only a servant, too.

CINDERELLA: But . . . the Prince . . .

PRINCE: Don't worry about him. I expect he'll . . . *(To DANDINI.)*
blow!

DANDINI: But you've got the horn, your High . . .

PRINCE: Herrumph! I'm sure the *Prince* will . . . *get lost* . . . in a
minute . . .

DANDINI: What? Oh. Ah! See what you mean. *(Grandly.)* I shall
be . . . over there, Your . . . Dandini . . . *(He goes.)*

PRINCE: *(To CINDERELLA)* But tell me . . . Could you love a
servant?

CINDERELLA: When I fall in love it won't matter to me whether he's rich or
poor . . . a servant or a . . .

PRINCE: A prince?

CINDERELLA: *(Laughing)* He isn't likely to be a prince . . .

GLADYS: *(Off)* There he is . . .

GERTRUDE: *(Off)* After him . . .

GLADYS: *(Off)* Tantivy, tantivy . . . ! Yoiks! Tallyho!

GERTRUDE: *(Off, calling)* Oh, Princey . . . !

GLADYS: *(Calling)* Your Highball . . . ?

DANDINI: *(Entering at a run and hiding from them)* Help!

CINDERELLA: *(Terrified)* Oh no! They mustn't find me here. I . . . I must
go . . .

*(She runs off as **(LXQ.16)** GLADYS and GERTRUDE enter.)*

PRINCE: Wait! *(Following, collides with the SISTERS.)*

GLADYS: Who're you telling to wait?

GERTRUDE: *(Pushing the PRINCE)* Yeh. Watch it, pleb . . . We're
                looking for the Prince . . .

GLADYS: *(Also pushing him)* So! Lead us to his lordship, laddie.

GERTRUDE: Hescort hus to his Highness, you horrible little flunkey,
                you!

PRINCE: Ah. *(Hauling DANDINI out.)* Here is the Prince, ladies.

DANDINI: Thanks a bunch . . .

PRINCE: *(Trying to leave)* Be my guest . . .

GERTRUDE: *(Catching him)* Here. Wait a minute though. How do you
                address a Prince?

GLADYS: He's already dressed.

PRINCE: You should curtsey very low and say something witty and
                clever. I'll leave you to it . . . *(He goes off through the
                woods.)*

                *(GERTRUDE curtseys very low – with ratchet noises from
                the pit.)*

GLADYS: Go on then. Say something witty and clever.

GERTRUDE: Watcher cock!

GLADYS: Don't say "cock". Say your Grace.

GERTRUDE: For what we are about to receive . . .

GLADYS: Oh, get out of the way. *(Grabbing DANDINI.)* Let a raver
                get a crack at the royal!

GERTRUDE: *(Also grabbing DANDINI)* Yeh. Come here, Princey. Don't
                play hard to get. You men are all alike . . .

GLADYS: *(Grabbing him back)* Yeh. Men are all I like too. Tell me . . .
                Don't you find my features . . . unusual?

DANDINI: Well yes. Not many people look like their passport photos.

GLADYS: My name's Gladys but you can call me Glad – as in Glad to meet you.

GERTRUDE: And I'm Gertrude . . . You can call me Gert and leave the rude bit 'til later . . .

GLADYS: *(Clasping DANDINI'S hand to her bosom)* Nay sir, la, sir – feel my heart –
How hard and fast it's beating.
Am I not struck with Cupid's dart?

DANDINI: No – just the central heating.

GERTRUDE: *(Trying hard for posh)* Hi hear has your Highness has ha hurge to get hitched hand has hit happens, *hie* his heager for ha husband.

GLADYS: Personally, I'd prefer a bachelor. Just look at my complexion, your Principality. I has a skin like a peach.

GERTRUDE: But who wants to go out with a forty-year-old peach?

GLADYS: Forty? I'm just about to come of age.

GERTRUDE: Yeh. The stone age.

GLADYS: You're so old, the calves of your legs have become cows.

GERTRUDE: And you're so ugly . . .

DANDINI: Ladies . . . ! Ladies?

GLADYS: Oh. Sorry, your Highness. *(Pulling him one way.)* He's mine . . .

GERTRUDE: *(Pulling him the other)* I saw him first . . . HE'S MINE!!

DANDINI: *(Escaping and running off)* Help!

GLADYS: After him. He's mine . . . !

GERTRUDE: Oh no he's not! He's mine . . . !

                (They exit in pursuit, fighting. (LXQ.17; SQ.5) The PRINCE and CINDERELLA enter.)

PRINCE: But – if he *were* to be a prince?

CINDERELLA: If I loved him, it wouldn't matter *what* he was.

PRINCE: And . . . could you love someone like me?

CINDERELLA: Someone like you?

PRINCE: Would you . . . could you . . . love me?

CINDERELLA: I know nothing about you. Yet . . .

PRINCE: Yet . . . ?

CINDERELLA: Yet . . . something tells me that I could love you very much.

(LXQ.18; FSQ.8)

        Song: SEARCHING FOR LOVE *(PRINCE and CINDERELLA)*

CINDERELLA: ALL THROUGH MY LIFE –
            AGAIN AND AGAIN –

PRINCE: SEARCHING FOR SOMEONE
            BUT SEARCHING IN VAIN.

BOTH: NOW, IN THIS MOMENT, IT'S TRUE –
            MY LONG QUEST IS OVER
            NOW I HAVE MET YOU.

            I'VE BEEN SEARCHING FOR LOVE –
            FOR THIS MOMENT OF BLISS –
            IN THIS MAGICAL PLACE,
            I TREMBLE FOR YOUR KISS
            AND I GLADLY SURRENDER
            TO LIPS WARM AND TENDER.
            THOUGH MY HEART NEVER KNEW,
            I'VE BEEN SEARCHING FOR YOU!

(LXQ.19; FSQ.8A)

GERTRUDE: *(Off)* Yoiks! Halooo! We're after youuuu!

CINDERELLA: I must go . . . *(She moves to leave.)*

PRINCE: *(Holding her)* Please wait. Where do you live?

CINDERELLA: I can't tell you that . . .

BARON: *(Off)* The wolf! The wolf!

SISTERS: *(Off)* We're off . . . ! WE'RE OFF!

PRINCE: Please . . .

CINDERELLA: *(Breaking free)* No. No . . . Goodbye . . . *(She runs off.)*

PRINCE: *(Exits, pursuing)* Wait . . . !

(LXQ.20)

SISTERS: Tantivy. Tantivy. Tantivy!

              (BUTTONS, the BARON and the SISTERS canter in on hobbyhorses.)

BARON: But the wolf just broke cover in the west.

GERTRUDE: That's why we're taking cover in the east.

BARON: But we've got to catch him. Or there'll be more dead chickens and lost sheep and mad cows.

GLADYS: Mad cows?

BARON: Well they'll be very very cross.

GERTRUDE: Did you perceive the Prince turn pale with passion when I pranced in his proximity? *(Prancing.)*

BUTTONS: That wasn't passion that was panic.

GLADYS: I thought I made a very good impression.

BUTTONS: The trouble with both of you is you've not got no etiquette.

GERTRUDE: Whatiquette?

BUTTONS: Etiquette. See? You don't even know what it is, do you?

GERTRUDE: Course I do! Etiquette – we give it to our cat.

BUTTONS: Not kit-e-kat! Etiquette is doing the proper thing properly.
              For example, out on the hunt, you should drink a toast to
              the Prince.

GLADYS: A toast to the Prince?

BUTTONS: I'll show you. Charge your glasses!

              (Music.   They ride forward and the cloth flies in **(FlyQ.4;
              LXQ.21)** *for:)*

                              Scene Four

*A Country Lane. They form a line with GLADYS at the R, then GERTRUDE,
then the BARON and with BUTTONS at the L.   The BARON fills up the
glasses as they form a line – from Right to Left, BUTTONS, GLADYS,
GERTRUDE, BARON.*

GERTRUDE: What do we do now?

BUTTONS: *(Raising glass)* Watch me: THE PRINCE, THE PRINCE!
              WE DRINK A TOAST,
              THE PRINCE IS HERE TODAY!
              WE DRINK A TOAST
              WE BOAST THE MOST
              AND SHOUT A LOUD
              HOORAY!

              *(At the end of the toast, they all throw the wine over their
              right shoulders into GLADYS'S face.)*

GLADYS: *(Furious)* Change places . . .

              *(Riding music as they all trot and canter about, changing
              positions, ending up GERTRUDE, BARON, BUTTONS,
              GLADYS.   They repeat the toast and all throw the contents
              of their glasses over their right shoulders, drenching
              GERTRUDE.)*

GERTRUDE: *(Furious)* Change places . . .

              *(Riding music as they all trot and canter about, changing
              positions, ending up BARON, BUTTONS, GLADYS,
              GERTRUDE.   They repeat the toast and all throw the
              contents of their glasses over their right shoulders,
              drenching the BARON.)*

BARON: That's not fair. Change places . . .

                    *(Riding music as they all trot and canter about, changing
                    positions, ending up BUTTONS, GLADYS, GERTRUDE,
                    BARON. The BARON and the SISTERS exchange glances –
                    smirk – going to get their own back. They repeat the
                    toast, during which BUTTONS trots round the back of the
                    line to place himself on the left. They complete the toast
                    and all throw the contents of their glasses over their right
                    shoulders, drenching GLADYS. BUTTONS mimes
                    innocence but they all spur their horses in a fury and chase
                    him off. As they canter off, (LXQ.22; FSQ.9) the PRINCE
                    and CINDERELLA appear in separate spots, looking for
                    each other.)*

PRINCE: It's no use . . . I've lost her . . . Was she nothing more than
                    a dream?

                    Song: Reprise of Duet

BOTH: I'VE BEEN SEARCHING FOR LOVE –
                    FOR THIS MOMENT OF BLISS –
                    IN THIS MAGICAL PLACE,
                    I TREMBLE FOR YOUR KISS
                    AND I GLADLY SURRENDER
                    TO LIPS WARM AND TENDER.
                    THOUGH MY HEART NEVER KNEW,
                    I'VE BEEN SEARCHING FOR YOU!

                    (Lights fade to blackout.)   *(LXQ.23; FSQ.9A; FlyQ.5)*

(LXQ.24)

                              Scene Five

*The Interior of BUTTONS' Toy Shop. There are toys and teddy bears
hanging up and on shelves everywhere. A workbench with various
oversize tools – including a big rubber hammer and a monkey wrench. A
huge chest of drawers. Large (living) dolls – Soldiers, a Ballerina, Dutch
dolls, Woodentop dolls, etc, lean in boxes against the walls. BUTTONS is
at his workbench, nailing a blonde doll's head onto a teddy's body.*

BUTTONS: Oh I'm so busy. *(Yawning.)* So much to do. And I'm that
                    tired I couldn't pip a grape. Hardly know what I'm doing.
                    Toys, toys, toys. Got to get 'em ready for Christmas, see.
                    And it's no sooner Christmas over than it's birthdays all the
                    year round and then it's Christmas again . . . There now . . .
                    (He holds up the teddy/doll.) Now that doesn't look quite

right to me. Can you see what's wrong with it? *(The AUDIENCE tell him.)* Oh. You're right. Aren't I daft? That tired, see . . . proper pooped . . . *(Yawns.)* I'll fix it later when I've had a bit of a kip. D'you know . . . 'S daft really, but . . . when I'm asleep – I do sometimes dream that all the toys come to life, see . . . Daft, innit? I mean toys can't come to life, can they? Toys is just . . . well . . . dummies!

(A number of DOLLS turn their heads and look at him crossly.)

BUTTONS: Still . . . *(Yawns.)* It's no use. I shall have to have some shut-eye. *(He pulls out bottom drawer and climbs in.)* Nighty nighty.

DOLLS: Pyjama pyjama.

(BUTTONS double takes then falls instantly asleep.)

GLADYS: *(Bellowing, off)* Buttons . . .

GERTRUDE: *(Tearfully, off)* Buttons . . . ?

GLADYS: I'll dead-arm you. I'll Chinese-burn you! I'll spifflicate you!

(The UGLIES enter, fighting. GERTRUDE is clutching bits of a torn teddy.)

GERTRUDE: Waaaaahhh! You beast. She's a beast, Buttons . . .

GLADYS: *(Lopes about snorting and grunting)* Herh, herh, herh!

GERTRUDE: *(In his ear)* BUTTONS!

BUTTONS: *(Leaps up)* What? Who? Where? Oh no! Not you two!

GERTRUDE: Look what she did done! *(Wails.)* Waaaahhh!

GLADYS: Don't care!

GERTRUDE: Don't care was made to care! *(Hits GLADYS with hammer from BUTTONS' workbench.)*

GLADYS: Ooooh, you! Just for that, I'll . . . *(She grabs a spanner from the bench – threatening.)*

BUTTONS: Will you stop it?

GERTRUDE: Oh no you won't!

BUTTONS: Give it a rest.

GLADYS: Oh yes I will!

BUTTONS: SHUT *UP!* Now what are you fighting about this time?

GERTRUDE: She – her – *it* – 'er tore my teddy. WAAAAHHHH!!!!

GLADYS: I never!

GERTRUDE: *(Hit with hammer)* You did!

GLADYS: *(Hit with monkey wrench)* Didn't!

GERTRUDE: *(Hit)* Did!

GLADYS: *(Hit)* Didn't!

GERTRUDE: *(Hit hit hit)* Did did did!

GLADYS: *(Hit hit hit)* Didn't didn't didn't!!!

                (A bell rings, off.)

BUTTONS: Seconds out – round one!

                *(They drop the weapons and start boxing/wrestling. The
                MAJORDOMO enters, pompously, ringing a bell.)*

MAJORDOMO: Oyez! Oyez! Oyez!

BUTTONS: Oh yes?

MAJORDOMO: Am I in the area of 'Ardup 'All?

GLADYS: *(Has GERTRUDE in a Boston crab)* Look out. We are not
                alone.

GERTRUDE: *(Posh)* We halready 'as double glazing.

MAJORDOMO: I am the 'ighly 'onourable Mark de Spencer, Majordomo to
                His Royal 'igness, the Prince Charming.

                (The UGLIES scramble up.)

GERTRUDE: *(Curtseying)* The Prince . . .

GLADYS: Oh we know the Prince . . .

GERTRUDE: He's mad to go out with us . . .

MAJORDOMO: 'E'd 'ave to be.

GLADYS: *(Spitting copiously)* Is it a private, personal post-it on perfumed pink paper pining for my prompt and passionate reply?

GERTRUDE: No it's not. It's to say he wants me for a bride.

GLADYS: He wouldn't want *you* for a pet.

GERTRUDE: Cheek *(Thump.)*

MAJORDOMO: Quiet, everybody and listen to the news . . .

BUTTONS: Who does he think he is? Trevor MacDonald?

MAJORDOMO: The Prince 'as announced that 'e is to 'old a grand state ball and I am come to deliver the invitations. I need 'ardly say that the invitations are only for the very select few.

GERTRUDE: I'm very select.

GLADYS: And I've had a few.

GERTRUDE: What is it? Some sort of house party?

GLADYS: He's not Noel Edmunds, you know.

GERTRUDE: Well he's got a crinkly bottom.

MAJORDOMO: It is a proper ball and I do not mean a raffle. Long frocks and tarrarras is the order of the day. No riff raff.

GLADYS: Cheek!

MAJORDOMO: The Royal Ball is to celebrate the Prince's coming-of-age birthday.

GLADYS: Coming-of-age? What a coincidence. I'm looking forward to my twenty-first birthday too, you know . . .

GERTRUDE: You're facing the wrong way.

MAJORDOMO: *(Producing invitations)*   These are the invitations for the
'Ardup 'ousehold.   The 'Onourable Miss Gladys 'Ardup . . .

GLADYS: I is she.

MAJORDOMO: The 'Onourable Miss Gertrude 'Ardup?

GERTRUDE: 'S me! 'S me! 'S me!

BUTTONS: What about Cinderella?

MAJORDOMO: There is no such personage on my parchment. 'As she got a
posh frock?

BUTTONS: Well . . . No . . .

MAJORDOMO: Then she can't 'ave no invite.   Posh frocks is obligatory.   I
bid you good day . . . *(He exits.)*

BUTTONS: But . . .

GLADYS: Don't be batty, Buttons, *she* can't go!

GERTRUDE: The very idea!   Come, Glad – let us return to Hardup Hall . . .

GLADYS: To sort out our frocks for the Prince's Ball . . .

GERTRUDE: But there hain't no frock for silly Cinders!

GLADYS: She can stay home and clean the winders!

(They exit, cackling.)

BUTTONS: Those rotten sisters . . . and poor Cinderella.   But blow them
and their nasty tricks.   She *shall* go to the ball.   But she
hasn't got a dress . . . Where on earth could I get a dress for
her?   I could make her one!   That's it!   I make all the
clothes for the dolls.   Why shouldn't I make a dress for
Cinderella?   Oh . . . no . . . it's no use.   I'd never manage it
on my own.   I'd need help.   And the ball's tomorrow night.
I'd never get it done in time – unless I had *lots* of help.   Oh
well . . . It was a nice idea . . . Better get some sleep and
think about it in the morning . . . *(He climbs into drawer.)*
Nighty nighty . . .

DOLLS: Pyjama, pyjama . . .

(BUTTONS double takes, then blows out the light (LXQ.25)
and falls fast asleep.)

(Music – Dress Making Ballet. A top drawer opens
(FSQ.10) and a ball rolls across the stage. A box opens
and TWO TOY SOLDIERS marching in step, carrying a roll
of fabric (the skirt) emerge. One of them blows a bugle in
BUTTONS' ear. He wakes with a start. He sees the fabric,
takes it from them. A FAIRY comes to life, dancing out from
a gift box, and pushes a (live) DUMMY on wheels into the
centre of the room. As BUTTONS fits and sews the fabric,
the FAIRY waves her wand and the dress begins to take
shape. A DUTCH DOLL clog-dances in with fabric (the
bodice). A TEDDY BEAR enters, with more fabric (sleeves).
BUTTONS cuts (using a toy crocodile as scissors) and sews
and makes the dress on the MODEL. When it is finished,
the MODEL comes to life and dances with him as the cloth
flies in for:)

(LXQ.26; FlyQ.6)

Scene Six

Outside Hardup Hall – Tradesman's Entrance.

BUTTONS: Cinderella . . . Cinderella . . . You *shall* go to the ball. All
             I've got to do now is get you an invitation and we'll show
             those ugly sisters . . .

             (The dance whirls to a triumphant finish. Blackout.)

(LXQ.27; FSQ.10A; FlyQ.7)   (LXQ.28)

Scene Seven

The UGLY SISTERS' Boudoir. Dressing-tables either side, stool for each.
Door UC.

The SISTERS are in corsets and horrible underwear, faces covered with
cream, hair in mountains of curlers. GLADYS is picking her toes and filing
the nails with a huge file. GERTRUDE is rummaging through a basket of
awful underwear.

SISTERS: *(Singing – to "Home on the Range")* We're off to the ball
             Where the men are so tall –

Where the wine flows and candlelight flickers.
We're going to get dressed
In our elegant best . . .

GERTRUDE: *(Looking through a huge pair of bloomers)* But I've got a hole in my knickers!

GLADYS: Here Gertie. Will you lace up my corset?

GERTRUDE: Is it corset time already?

GLADYS: Corset is.

GERTRUDE: Right. Breathe in. *(Putting her foot in GLADYS'S back and pulling.)*

GLADYS: Oh just think of all the people we'll meet at the ball. Fergy'll be there – Sir Cliff – Tony Blair . . .

GERTRUDE: Yes yes yes. I can see him now doing his tap dancing.

GLADYS: That's Lionel Blair . . . OW! Do you mind? You're pulling in *all* the wrong places. After all, I has a hourglass figure . . .

GERTRUDE: But all the sand's run to the bottom. There. Now. My turn. *(Holds the corset as an accordian and sings.)* "Just one Cornetto . . ."

GLADYS: Shut up. And breathe in. *(Putting her foot in GERTRUDE'S back.)* I said breathe in – breathe in!

GERTRUDE: *(Strangulated)* I *am* breathing in!

GLADYS: Well breathe in better! Like trying to tie up a parcel of tripe. There. Is that comfortable?

GERTRUDE: *(High pitched)* Oh yes – lovely.

GLADYS: Marvellous. *(Wiping off cream.)* Now – the makeup!

GERTRUDE: The makeup!

GLADYS: *(Producing a huge lipstick)* Will you do my lips, Gert? You have to get the line just right to show off their enigmatic sensuality . . .

GERTRUDE: Keep still then . . . Pucker up . . .

(GLADYS puckers grotequely.)

GERTRUDE: *(Hitting her in the mouth with the lipstick, making a large round blotch)* There. Perfect! *(Wiping cream off her face.)* Now you'll have to do the rest yourself or I shall never be ready.

GLADYS: Alright but just pass me the talc.

GERTRUDE: *(Throws glad a huge canister labelled VIM)* To you . . .

GLADYS: To me . . . Tell me, why do you put that cream on your face?

GERTRUDE: To make myself beautiful.

GLADYS: Doesn't work though, does it?

GERTRUDE: CHEEK! *(She starts to do her lips.)*

GLADYS: *(Throwing Vim under her arms)* For under-arm charm, please *him* – with *vim*.

GERTRUDE: *(Incomprehensible, still doing lips)* Ham hoo hock a hohog gog?

GLADYS: *(Outraged)* I beg yours?

GERTRUDE: Ha heh han hoo hock a hohog gog?

GLADYS: *(Hits her)* How dare you?

GERTRUDE: Ouch! What was that for?

GLADYS: For what you called me.

GERTRUDE: HI haid . . . "have you got a cotton bud?"

GLADYS: Oh! *(Huge cotton bud.)* To you . . .

GERTRUDE: To me . . .

GLADYS: And pass me that Brillo pad – my nails need doing.

GERTRUDE: *(Passes her a huge brillo pad)* To you . . . *(Then cleans her ears elaborately with the cotton bud.)*

GLADYS: To me . . .

GERTRUDE: And now . . . le parfoom! (*A huge flit spray labelled "Le Harpic".*) When the Prince gets a whiff of this he'll swoon at my feet.

GLADYS: I can believe it, it's making me feel sick from here.

GERTRUDE: Try a bit. It attracts men like flies . . .

GLADYS: But I don't like men like flies. (*She picks up a pair of road cones.*)

GERTRUDE: What are those for?

GLADYS: (*Fixing them to her chest*) Sillycone implants. Eat your heart out, Madonna.

GERTRUDE: (*Rhapsodic*) Oh . . . I'll never forget the first time I did meet the Prince. 'Twas on top of the suspension bridge.

GLADYS: She was dangling her feet in the water at the time.

GERTRUDE: (*Dreamy*) He did give to I a flower. (*GLADYS gives her a huge flower.*) And he did say "Here's one bloom". Then he did give to I another flower. (*GLADYS gives her another flower.*) And he did say "Here's two blooms. Now you've got a pair of bloomers."

GLADYS: I think I shall wear my eighteen carrat gold necklace . . .

GERTRUDE: Eighteen carrats?

GLADYS: (*Necklace of golden carrots*) Mmmm – Littlewoods catalogue – page twenty six.

GERTRUDE: I went out with my boyfriend last night – us went to Ritzy's and then us . . . went home.

GLADYS: Did the earth move for you?

GERTRUDE: No but the dressing table twitched a few times.

BUTTONS: (*Enters*) Hello girls.

GLADYS: Where? Oh, its you Buttons – you silly little man.

BUTTONS: Listen, I've had enough of this little man bit. I'm big. I'm butch. I'm known as the Mike Tyson of Tockington round here.

GERTRUDE: Big and butch!   You couldn't blow the skin off a rice
                 pudding.

GLADYS: You couldn't lift a lettuce leaf.

BUTTONS: Oh couldn't I?   Watch this . . . *(He tears a telephone
                 directory in half.)* Well?

GERTRUDE: I was still reading that.

BUTTONS: I thought you two were off to the beauty parlour.

GERTRUDE: We've been.

BUTTONS: Was it shut?

GLADYS: How dare you? Now leave us. We've got to get our hair
                 done for the ball.

BUTTONS: Ah well I've got just the thing for you girls.   It's my new
                 invention. It's my instant permanent prinking and perming
                 appliance – as used at the Dog of the Year Show!

GLADYS: Well let's try it.

BUTTONS: *(Aside, going)* Now's my chance to get my own back . . .

GLADYS: I just can't decide what dress to wear. *(She holds up a
                 dress against herself.)*

GERTRUDE: Where did you get that from? Colourblind 'R' Us? *I* shall
                 wear a dress to match my eyes.

GLADYS: Wherever would you get a bloodshot dress?

BUTTONS: *(Entering, pushing the machine)* Now then – this machine
                 will guarantee you fine, rich, silky, luxuriant, dandruff-free
                 hair all down your back – none on your head – just down
                 your back . . .

GERTRUDE: Well, I don't know! What does us have to do, Buttons?

BUTTONS: You put your head in here and the machine does the rest. I
                 pour in the styling gel. Pump it up a bit and before you can
                 say, Dawn Carmenrolla . . . you'll be as stylish as Sharon
                 Stone . . .

GLADYS: Oh shall we, Gert? I shall look like Naomi Campbell or
               Chrissy Brinkley . . .

GERTRUDE: More like Hinckley point. You first.

BUTTONS: Well fortunately, what I have here is the double-barnet
               deluxe whereby I can do two for the price of one. *(He opens
               it up – brings out striped rabbit.)* I wondered where I'd
               put that.

GLADYS: Brilliant. Let's go for it.

BUTTONS: It's not cheap.

GERTRUDE: Money is no object – as long as it's free.

BUTTONS: Just place your bonces in the box. *(They put their heads in.
               He closes the lid and pulls a lever. The machine starts to
               hum and vibrate.) (SQ.6)* Comfy? Now I pour in the
               shampoo . . . *("Wash 'n' Go".)* And now the secret
               ingredient . . . *("Go and Wash".)* Now for the steam
               treatment . . . *(He inserts hose – jets of smoke.)*

GLADYS: *(Muffled)* I don't think I like this . . .

GERTRUDE: I'm not sure this is a good idea . . .

GLADYS: Hot hot hot . . .

GERTRUDE: Oh . . . Mummy . . . ! Mummy, Mummy . . . !

BUTTONS: It's alright. I think you're done . . .

               *(Bells ring, whistle, klaxon, BANG! He lifts the lid and
               they stagger out in gigantic, spiky, neon-coloured fright
               wigs sticking up all over the place and with smoke pouring
               out.)*

GLADYS: Well, I must say, Buttons, that really does feel as if it's put
               the life back into my hair . . .

GERTRUDE: Yes it feels so thick and bouncy I could just . . .

               (They turn and see each other.)

BOTH: AAAAAHHHH! We're on fire . . . We're frizzled and
               frazzled!

BUTTONS: Never fear – Buttons is here! *(He squirts them with the
                soda syphon.)*

SISTERS: WAAAAAHHHH!!!!

                (Blackout.)   *(LXQ.29; FlyQ.8)*

(LXQ.30; FSQ.11)

Scene Eight

The Kitchen of Hardup Hall.

Song: ONCE YOU LOSE YOUR HEART *(CINDERELLA)*

CINDERELLA: ONCE YOU LOSE YOUR HEART,
             ONCE SOMEBODY TAKES IT
             FROM THE PLACE IT RESTED IN BEFORE.
             ONCE YOU LOSE YOUR HEART –
             ONCE SOMEBODY WAKES IT,
             THEN IT ISN'T YOUR HEART ANYMORE.
             IT'S GONE BEFORE YOU KNEW IT COULD EVER GO THAT
                                              WAY –
             AND NOW YOU MUST PURSUE IT FOR EVER AND A DAY.
             ONCE YOU LOSE YOUR HEART,
             ONCE SOMEBODY TAKES IT,
             THERE'S ONE THING CERTAIN FROM THE START –
             YOU'LL FIND FOR EVER –
             YOU'VE GOT TO FOLLOW YOUR HEART.

(LXQ.31; FSQ.11A)

BARON: *(Entering)* Oh, Cinders, you look so sad . . . I'm so sorry.

CINDERELLA: It doesn't matter, Daddy. It's just that I would so like to go
             to the ball and I did so hope that Gladys or Gertrude might
             lend me a dress. They have so many, after all.

BARON: You don't have to tell me. I got the bill for every one of
                them. But I told them to lend you one, Cinderella. I burst
                into their boudoir and put my foot down.

CINDERELLA: And?

BARON: They stamped on it – both of them – twice. I'm *so* sorry.

CINDERELLA: Oh please stop saying you're sorry. It isn't your fault. You'd better go. They'll be waiting for you to take them . . . *(Weeping.)* To the ball . . .

BARON: Yes. Well. Goodnight . . . *(He goes sadly.)*

(BUTTONS enters with the dress and an invitation. He hides the dress and holds the invitation behind his back.)

BUTTONS: Come on, Cinders, hurry up. You'll be late.

CINDERELLA: Late? Late for what?

BUTTONS: For the ball, of course.

CINDERELLA: Oh, Buttons, it isn't like you to be unkind. You know I can't go to the ball . . . I haven't got a dress . . .

BUTTONS: Oh yes you have . . .

CINDERELLA: Don't be silly, Buttons. And I haven't got an invitation . . .

BUTTONS: *(Producing invitation)* Oh yes you have . . . Here. I went and saw that Majordomo and got you one special . . .

(BUTTONS sneaks off for the dress as:)

CINDERELLA: *(Reading)* His Royal Highness, the Prince Charming requests the pleasure of . . . the Honourable Miss Cinderella Hardup . . . at his grand Coming-of-age Ball . . . Oh, Buttons! Buttons?

BUTTONS: *(Emerging with the dress)* And look. My friends and me made you a dress. I'm not sure it's quite the height of fashion but . . .

CINDERELLA: Oh, Buttons, it's lovely . . .

BUTTONS: And you'll be the loveliest girl there, Cinders. Now hurry up and get ready . . .

CINDERELLA: *(Hugging him)* Oh, Buttons!! Lovely Buttons . . . !

GERTRUDE: *(Sweeps in in her cape, singing)* "I feel pretty! Oh so pretty . . ." *(Stops short.)* And what's going on here?

BUTTONS: Cinders is just going to get ready to go to the ball.

GERTRUDE: But she isn't going to the ball.

BUTTONS: That's where you're wrong, Face-ache. Cinders *is* going to the ball.

GERTRUDE: She can't. She's not got no dress . . .

BUTTONS: Oh yes she has. Look . . .

GLADYS: *(Also sweeps in her cape, singing)* "I'm lovely . . . Absolutely lovely . . . I'm so . . ." *(Stops short.)* What's all this then?

CINDERELLA: Look, Gladys. Buttons made me this beautiful dress – so that I can go to the ball . . .

GLADYS: But you can't go without an invitation.

CINDERELLA: But dear Buttons went to the palace specially and got me an invitation.

BUTTONS: And all I've got to do now is go and get her shoes . . . Back in a tick . . . *(He exits.)*

GLADYS: So . . . you've got a beautiful dress, Cinders . . .

CINDERELLA: Yes, Gladys . . .

GLADYS: Let me have a look at it, there's a dear . . . *(She takes the dress from CINDERS and holds it up against herself.)*

GERTRUDE: And you've got an invitation too, Cinders . . .

CINDERELLA: Yes, Gertrude . . .

GERTRUDE: Let me have a look at it, you little sweetie, you . . .

CINDERELLA: It says my name – look . . .

GERTRUDE: *(Viciously)* So! Cinderella's got a dress, Gladys . . .

GLADYS: *(Viciously)* Yes. And Cinderella's got an invitation too, Gertrude . . .

GERTRUDE: *(Ripping it slowly)* Not now she hasn't.

CINDERELLA: Gertrude! No! Please . . . !

BUTTONS: *(Enters with shoes)* What's going on?

GERTRUDE: *(Throwing the pieces into the fire)* Oh dear – clumsy me –
I've gone and burnt your invitation, Cinders . . .

GLADYS: *(Pulling pieces off the dress)* Yes and . . . Oh dear. You
didn't sew this dress very well, Buttons . . .

GERTRUDE: *(Ripping it)* No. It's just falling to pieces in our hands.

                (They scatter the fragments of dress over the floor.)

GLADYS: Oh dear . . .

BUTTONS: You horrible monsters . . . *(Chasing them, beating at them
with a broom.)*

SISTERS: *(Chanting)* No invitation and no dress at all –
Poor Cinderella can't go to the ball!
No invitation and no dress at all –
Poor Cinderella can't go to the ball!
Hee, hee hee and haa haa haa!
Now's the time to say TARRAH!

                *(BUTTONS chases them off. They go, cackling and
snorting nastily. **(LXQ.32)** CINDERELLA sinks down
beside the hearth and weeps.)*

BUTTONS: Oh, Cinders . . . Your lovely dress . . . and the invitation all
torn and burnt up in the fire . . . Just wait till I get hold of
those two, I'll . . . I'll . . . I'll get Lennox Lewis onto it.

CINDERELLA: It doesn't matter, Buttons. It was only a dream. I couldn't
have gone anyway. I've got too much to do. It would have
been lovely though . . . to go to . . . a real ball . . .

BUTTONS: Don't worry. It happens to some of the most famous
people.

CINDERELLA: What do you mean?

BUTTONS: Well, even Beckham misses the ball sometimes.

CINDERELLA: Aw, Buttons, come and sit with me by the fire . . .

BUTTONS: Did you know that Catherine the grate got her name by
sitting by the fireplace?

CINDERELLA: *(Tries to laugh)* Oh, Buttons.

BUTTONS: That's right. Laugh . . . I'll tell you what. We'll have our
              own ball right here.

CINDERELLA: Don't be silly.   I haven't anything to wear – not even for a
              kitchen ball . . .

BUTTONS: You couldn't look lovelier than you do now, Cinders. You'd
              look lovely in anything. I can just see you in a silver tiara –
              in a dress with a long swishy train.

CINDERELLA: Oh, Buttons . . .

BUTTONS: All you have to do is . . . believe.

              (Music.) *(LXQ.33; FSQ.12)*

BUTTONS: *(Taking the tablecloth and fixing it round her waist)*
              Here's your long dress, Modom. *(Taking the spatula from
              the pan.)*   And here's the fan you desired . . . You'll need
              some delicate little dancing slippers – and here they are.
              (Putting huge wellies onto her feet.)

CINDERELLA: *(Joining in)* My diamonds. I shall need my diamonds.

BUTTONS: I'll fetch them from the safe this minute . . . *(He hangs a
              string of onions round her neck, cherries from a bowl for
              ear-rings.)*

CINDERELLA: My cape . . . The evening is chilly . . .

BUTTONS: Your cape . . . *(Picking up the hearthrug and fixing it to
              her back.)* And *(Placing a cake-frill on her head.)* your
              tiara . . . There now . . . you're every inch the Royal
              Princess . . . And I'm . . . *(He puts a saucepan on his head.)*
              a soldier . . . *(Stepping into the coalscuttles as boots.)* A
              dashing cavalier! *(Two oven gloves as gauntlets.)* A death-
              or-glory dragoon! *(An apron as a cape.)*   The Captain of
              your Imperial Guard . . .

              Song: SPREAD A LITTLE HAPPINESS *(Duet) (BUTTONS
              and CINDERELLA)*

BUTTONS: I'VE GOT A CREED
              FOR EV'RY NEED
              SO EASY THAT IT MUST SUCCEED;

I'LL SET IT DOWN FOR YOU TO READ –
SO PLEASE TAKE HEED.
KEEP OUT THE GLOOM!
LET IN THE SUN!
THAT'S MY ADVICE TO EV'RYONE.
IT'S ONLY ONCE WE PASS THIS WAY –
SO DAY BY DAY:

EVEN WHEN THE DARKEST CLOUD IS IN THE SKY,
YOU MUSTN'T SIGH
AND YOU MUSTN'T CRY;
JUST SPREAD A LITTLE HAPPINESS AS YOU GO BY –

CINDERELLA: I'LL TRY!

BUTTONS: WHAT'S THE USE OF WORRYING AND FEELING BLUE?
WHEN DAYS ARE LONG, KEEP ON SMILING THROUGH
AND SPREAD A LITTLE HAPPINESS TILL DREAMS COME
TRUE.

CINDERELLA: SURELY I'D BE WISE TO MAKE THE BEST OF EV'RY
BLUES DAY;

BUTTONS: DON'T YOU REALISE YOU'LL FIND NEXT MONDAY OR
NEXT TUESDAY –

BOTH: YOUR/MY GOLDEN SHOES DAY?

EVEN WHEN THE DARKEST CLOUDS ARE IN THE SKY,
YOU MUSTN'T SIGH
AND YOU MUSTN'T CRY;
JUST SPREAD A LITTLE HAPPINESS AS YOU GO BY!

(They dance and end up laughing and collapsing beside the fire.)

(LXQ.34; FSQ.12A)

CINDERELLA: *(Laughter fading)* It's no good, Buttons, we're just
pretending. I'll never be able to go to a real ball – we both
know it.

BUTTONS: We'll have to make do with a banquet then. I know, I'll go
and get some fish and chips and we'll stay here and watch
Emmerdale.

(There is a knock at the door, off.)

CINDERELLA: Now who can that be at this time of night?

BUTTONS: *(Going to see who it is)* If it's those sisters come back because they've forgotten something, I'll lock 'em in the coal cellar . . .

FAIRY: *(Entering)* May I come in, my dear, I'm frozen quite through to the marrow . . .

CINDERELLA: Why, it's the old lady I met in the woods . . . Oh dear – you poor creature – come into the warm . . .

BUTTONS: Yes. Come and sit down by the fire . . .

FAIRY: You seem upset, my dear. Have you been crying?

CINDERELLA: Oh . . . It's nothing . . .

FAIRY: Nay, cry no more nor sigh no more but dry your tears, my
                                                              dear
            I come to bless your happiness – to guard and guide you
                                                  through the year . . .

CINDERELLA: You poor old thing . . . don't worry about me . . . In any case – I don't mean to be unkind but . . . what can you do?

            (A clock chimes.)

FAIRY: Hark, Cinderella – the magic hour
            A time of wonder for you, my dear –
            For I am a creature of fairy power
            To make your dreams come true. See here!

            (She throws off her cloak and stands resplendent.)
            (FSQ.13)

BUTTONS: Flippin' heck! That's cool.

CINDERELLA: But . . . who *are* you?

FAIRY: I am your Fairy Godmother, Cinderella. My happy task to care for you throughout these unhappy times, to lead you safely through the years of tears to the happiness and joy which await you.

CINDERELLA: Await me? Where?

FAIRY: Make haste, Cinderella, your Prince waits for you –

Surely you hear his call.
Make haste, for all that I tell you is true –
And tonight you shall go to the Royal Ball.

CINDERELLA: But I can't go to the ball – my sisters tore up my invitation
and burnt it.

FAIRY: Then we must mend it and fetch it from the fire.
(Waving her wand.) Let torn up fragments be again entire!

(The invitation, intact, glides out of the fire.)

BUTTONS: *(Catching it)* Now that's what I call a special delivery . . .
But how *can* she go? I made her a dress but those meanies
tore it into pieces. And how would she get there . . . ?

(Music.) *(LXQ.35)*

FAIRY: Bring all that I command and ask no questions . . .

BUTTONS: But . . .

FAIRY: No buts – no doubting – no suggestions.
Fetch me that pumpkin by the door
It shall be your carriage – lay it down there – on the kitchen
floor.
We'll need some horses . . .

BUTTONS: Horses? For a pumpkin?

FAIRY: Now let me see.
Go to the mousetraps and set all free
And bring them here for they shall be
The prettiest ponies in history.

*(BUTTONS and CINDERS rush about as they are told [The
substitute CINDERS takes over during this].)*

FAIRY: See that lizard basking by the grate –
He'll be your coachman as you drive in state.
And, last of all bring me two white rats . . .

BUTTONS: White rats? But where am I going to find . . .

*(There is a Flash (PyroQ.3; LXQ.36) and two white rats
appear.)*

FAIRY: There! In braided coats and feathered hats,
They shall be your servants to open the door

And keep your train from sweeping the floor . . .
For a gown like yours was never seen
On duchess, princess or royal queen.
No more a servant ill-used by all –
But the belle of the Prince's birthday ball!

*(A Flash **(PyroQ.4; LXQ.37; FSQ.14)** and CINDERELLA
is transformed. [The substitute BUTTONS takes over at
this point].)*

FAIRY: May this be Cinderella's night
                Let wonder set the skies alight –
                May all my magic speed her flight
                And bear her to the hall.
                Her fairy coach, this pumpkin make,
                Driver and footmen for her sake
                These mice as horses now I take –
                She *shall* go to the ball
                Ring out the bells throughout the nation

                (Bells peal joyfully.)

FAIRY: Let all be joy and jubilation
                As I summon up a transformation
                Which changes all!

                *(The Scene transforms **(LXQ.38; FlyQ.9; SQ.7)** into:)*

                            Scene Nine

*The Fairy Forest. The walls dissolve to become glittering trees, foliage
grows up from the ground and down from above. The Carriage, ponies
and FAIRY ATTENDANTS appear. A Flash **(PyroQ.5)** and BUTTONS is
changed into white uniform with gold trimmings.*

(LXQ.39; FSQ.13A & 14A)

                Song: ACT ONE FINALE *(FAIRY, BUTTONS, CINDERELLA,
                FAIRIES)*

FAIRY: O, DEAREST GIRL,
                YOUR MISERY IS ENDED.
                AND SO, TONIGHT, A PRINCESS YOU SHALL REIGN.
                GO TO THE BALL!
                FOR THERE, ALL-POWERFUL AND SPLENDID,
                LOVE WAITS TO CONQUER ALL –
                TO CONQUER ALL.

BUT THERE BEWARE THE SOUND OF MIDNIGHT
CHIMING –
THE SOUND OF MIDNIGHT CHIMING,
FOR, AT THAT HOUR, MY MAGIC WILL FORSAKE YOU
AND ALL THESE RICHES VANISH IN THIN AIR.
HEAR ME AGAIN – WHEN MIDNIGHT CHIMES ARE
PEALING – BEWARE!
FOR THEN MY MAGIC FADES AND ALL OF THIS WILL
VANISH.
THEN YOUR LOVELY DRESS WILL TURN TO RAGS!

(LXQ.40)

FAIRY & BUT NOW, DEPART!
CHORUS:

AND MAY THE MUSIC GLADDEN YOUR HEART.
THERE MAY YOU FIND TRUE LOVE!
THERE MAY YOU FIND TRUE LOVE!
WHERE YOUR PRINCE AWAITS, YOU'LL FIND TRUE
LOVE!

(The carriage moves forwards as the curtain falls.)

(LXQ.41; FSQ.13A & 14A)

ACT TWO

Scene One

The Ballroom of the Palace. **(LXQ.42)** *Music: a Polka. (DANDINI, LORDS and LADIES.) All (including DANDINI as the Prince) are dancing. DANDINI dances with great enthusiasm, whirling from one partner to another. The PRINCE himself stands alone and sad. At the end of the dance, DANDINI joins him.*

DANDINI: Not dancing, your Highness?

PRINCE: Who?

DANDINI: I mean . . . Dandini. Oh, honestly sire, we can't keep this up any longer. Can't I go back to being your servant again?

PRINCE: You can when I need once more to be the Prince. Don't pretend you're not enjoying yourself.

DANDINI: Oh no – time of my life . . . *(A lady curtseys to him, he bows low and is tempted to follow her.)* But join the dancing at least, your Dandiniship. There are some fair crackers here tonight, all curtseying and coquetting and I can fix you up with any you fancy.

PRINCE: They're very . . . attractive but . . . I can't get that one lovely face out of my memory . . .

DANDINI: The girl you met in the woods . . .

PRINCE: Where *is* she, Dandini – your Highness – where can she *be*? Why can't I find her – search as I might? I *had* hoped she would be among the guests tonight.

DANDINI: But she was a servant, sire, so surely not . . .

             (Fanfare.)

DANDINI: But look. Someone new is arriving . . .

PRINCE: Perhaps it might be her . . .

(LXQ.43)

MAJORDOMO: My lords, ladies and gentlemen – His Honour the Baron Hardup and his dishonourable daughters – Miss Gladys and Miss Gertrude.

(The BARON and the UGLIES appear at the top of the staircase.)

GLADYS: Yoo hoo . . . Princey . . . !

GERTRUDE: I is here at last, your Highflight. Has you missed me . . . ?

DANDINI: Oh no. Hide me . . .

PRINCE: Too late. I'll leave you to it . . .

GLADYS: I seed him first . . .

GERTRUDE: No you didn't . . . *(They fight, get tangled and roll down the stairs landing in a heap at DANDINI'S feet.)*

GLADYS: Oh, Your Highness! I've kept every dance for you.

GERTRUDE: Pay no attention to her, your Highstool.

GLADYS: *(Sings)* The man that I marry will have to be . . .

GERTRUDE: *(Sings)* As blind as a bat and a hundred and three . . .

GLADYS: And you know, I'm very talented. I think a princess needs to be *so* accomplished, don't you?

GERTRUDE: Oh yes she's very talented. She does farmyard impressions.

DANDINI: The sounds?

GERTRUDE: No, the smells. You know, your Highness, I just can't get you off my mind.

DANDINI: And I can't get you off my hands.

(Tango Music.)

GLADYS: O hark, your Highness – the tango . . . *(Grabbing him and whirling him away.)* You know – I've got dancing in my blood.

DANDINI: Your circulation must be bad then because it certainly hasn't reached your feet. *(The sisters snatch DANDINI and tango with him alternately until they end up tangoing together, scream and fall in a heap.)*

(Fanfare.)

MAJORDOMO: Your Royal Highness, my Lords and Ladies. The Princess Cenerentolla . . .

(LXQ.44; FSQ.15)

(CINDERELLA appears at the top of the stairs. All gasp.)

DANDINI: What a beautiful girl . . .

GERTRUDE: Oh thank you, your Highness . . .

DANDINI: Not you! Look . . .

GLADYS: Hmph! Wonder who *she* is? I could swear I've seen her in Sainsbury's . . .

GERTRUDE: I must say the fizzog looks funnily familiar . . .

(DANDINI approaches CINDERELLA but the PRINCE pushes past him, takes her hand and leads her down into the ballroom.)

(The Orchestra strikes up – "SEARCHING FOR LOVE". They begin to dance.)

GLADYS: Did you see that? Cheek of that flunkey – pushing the Prince out of the way like that!

MAJORDOMO: But that *is* the Prince. The other is Dandini – his valet.

GLADYS: His valet? A commoner? Well! Ever been had!

GERTRUDE: *(Sadly)* No.

PRINCE: *(To CINDERELLA)* Where have you been? I despaired of ever seeing you again. And is it true that you are a princess and not a servant after all?

CINDERELLA: I am not what I seem. I really don't know who – or what – I am . . . But does it matter?

PRINCE: Not at all.

CINDERELLA: But you are a prince and not a servant either?

PRINCE: And does *that* matter?

CINDERELLA: I told you when we met – if I loved someone, it wouldn't matter what he was – high or lowly – rich or poor . . .

BOTH: *(Sing)* AND I GLADLY SURRENDER
TO LIPS WARM AND TENDER.
THOUGH MY HEART NEVER KNEW –
I'VE BEEN SEARCHING FOR YOU!

(They dance off together, followed by the guests. GLADYS accosts a number of LORDS, all of whom decline to dance with her.)

(LXQ.45; FSQ.15A)

GLADYS: It's no use. There's not a man in the place with eyes for anybody other than that horrible hussy who came late.

GERTRUDE: Well, if we're not going to rumba with a Royal, I'm going to unclip me corsets and get in some grub.

GLADYS: Good idea. *(Calls.)* Service!

GERTRUDE: I say – you – yes, you! Any chance of getting a bite?

BUTTONS: *(Entering)* And where would you like to be bitten, Modom?

GERTRUDE: Gerroff! It's you! Zip fastener!

BUTTONS: Buttons.

GERTRUDE: What are you doing here?

BUTTONS: Earning an honest crust. It's two years since the Baron paid me any wages and the shop's not doing well in the recession so I'm "waiting" 'til something turns up.

GLADYS: But are you in the waiter's union?

BUTTONS: Oh yes. I'm a chop steward.

(He claps his hands. FOOTMEN bring on tables and chairs.)

GLADYS: Let's hope this place lives up to its name.

GERTRUDE: What? The Rumbling Tum?

GLADYS: That was me, you fool. Now what are we going to have?

GERTRUDE: Whatever's big and hot with plenty of it.

GLADYS: Sounds as if you'll want the Shirehampton Special, dear. I'm going to go for a delicacy. Cow pie.

GERTRUDE: Sounds appropriate.

GLADYS: Cheek. With the addition of some lumpy gravy, it'll be scrummy.

GERTRUDE: You don't need any more lumps, dear. Look at you – a walking Brent Knoll.

GLADYS: Just for that, I shan't sit with you. I shall sit here and you can sit on your tod at that table. *(They sit at separate tables.)* Now we must ring the bell for service.

GERTRUDE: *(Rings bell)*   Hey you – Velcro . . .

BUTTONS: Buttons.

GERTRUDE: Buttons. Could we have the menu?

BUTTONS: We don't have a menu. You name it – we've got it.

GERTRUDE: A rack of lamb . . .

BUTTONS: We haven't got it.

GERTRUDE: Fish and chips.

BUTTONS: We haven't got it.

GERTRUDE: Roast beef and two veg.

BUTTONS: We haven't got it.

GERTRUDE: I thought you said – you name it – we've got it.

BUTTONS: You haven't named it yet.

(GLADYS rings her bell.)

BUTTONS:	You rang ma'am? What would you like?
GLADYS:	I'd like the soup. What is it?
BUTTONS:	I've got chicken soup and pea soup.
GLADYS:	I'll have the chicken soup.
BUTTONS:	*(Calling)* One chicken soup . . .
VOICE:	*(Off)* One chicken soup . . .
GLADYS:	No I've changed my mind. I don't want chicken soup.
BUTTONS:	You don't?
GLADYS:	No. I want pea soup.
BUTTONS:	*(Calling)* Hold the chicken and make it pea.
GERTRUDE:	What goes with the soup, waiter?
BUTTONS:	A nice tongue sandwich.
GERTRUDE:	I dont eat anything that's come out of an animal's mouth.
BUTTONS:	How about a couple of eggs?
GERTRUDE:	Alright, I'll have the soup. What is it?
BUTTONS:	Runny.
GERTRUDE:	You stupid little man.
BUTTONS:	It is the soup of the day.
GERTRUDE:	Windsor?
BUTTONS:	No. Wednesday.
GERTRUDE:	I've changed my mind. I'll have a plover's egg pizza with oodles of runny cheese . . .
BUTTONS:	*(Calls)* Soup and egg pizza coming up.
GLADYS:	I hope not.

(BUTTONS exits. The UGLIES prepare their napkins – GERTRUDE gets the tablecloth tucked in.)

GERTRUDE: *(Calling)* And how long will my pizza be?

BUTTONS: *(Returning)* We only do round ones.

(BUTTONS plonks soup in front of GLADYS and pizza in front of GERTRUDE. GLADYS slurps soup, GERTRUDE sucks eggs.)

BUTTONS: Sounds like the Severn Bore coming up.

(GERTRUDE belches.)

BUTTONS: Pardon?

GERTRUDE: I didn't say anything.

BUTTONS: How nice to have quality customers.

GLADYS: Waiter! What's this fly doing in my soup?

BUTTONS: Looks like a backstroke to me.

GERTRUDE: *(Bouncing an egg on the table)* And what's wrong with this egg?

BUTTONS: Don't ask me – I only laid the table. *(To GLADYS.)* Everything alright, Modom?

GLADYS: Alright? Look at this. Now there's a City supporter *(Or other local football team.)* swimming in the soup.

BUTTONS: Well, you win some, you lose some, Modom.

GLADYS: Yes but he's playing away.

(BUTTONS produces a tiny fishing rod. He casts and winds and yanks out a little City supporter.)

GLADYS: Now I would like some Pastal. What have you got?

BUTTONS: We've got Fettoccini, Botticelli, Vermiccelli, Cantonati.

GERTRUDE: Fettocinni, Botticelli, Vermicelli, Cantonati?

GLADYS: What about spag bog?

BUTTONS: We've got the spag but we're out of bog.

GERTRUDE: Alright, let's have the spag but make it quick.

GLADYS: Yeh. Make it quick – you *little* man.

(BUTTONS flinches, goes and returns at once with a trolley with a big tureen of spaghetti to C stage. He grabs the soup plates and throws them into the wings. He puts a dollop of spaghetti on GLADYS'S plate and then crosses to put a big dollop on GERTRUDE'S. They are joined by long elastic. They start pulling and tugging 'til elastic is stretched. BUTTONS produces scissors and cuts it. Both get pinged. They eat their spaghetti with much slurping and belching. They wipe their mouths on the cloth. GERTRUDE sneezes into her meal.)

GERTRUDE: I'll have that bit later.

GLADYS: Now we need the pooding.

GERTRUDE: The pooding?

GLADYS: Yes. The pooding.

GERTRUDE: Poo – sounds a bit niffy to me.

GLADYS: What have you got, waiter?

BUTTONS: How about yoghourt?

GLADYS: Yoghourt? What do you think I am? A cissy?

BUTTONS: What about a gert jelly?

GERTRUDE: How gert?

BUTTONS: Gert as a sandcastle.

GERTRUDE: That's gert. What colour?

BUTTONS: Red – with dots.

GLADYS: We'll have it but make it quick.

BUTTONS: One quick jelly coming up.

(BUTTONS goes and returns, staggering, with a huge wobbly jelly. He gives it to GERTRUDE to hold – grabs spag plates, throws them into wings. The jelly (cold) passed between GERTRUDE. GLADYS and BUTTONS. It ends up with BUTTONS who goes off balance and vanishes, staggering into wings. A crash.)

BUTTONS: *(Returning)* Help! Help! We've lost the jelly . . . !

GERTRUDE: Lost the jelly?

GLADYS: Lost the jelly?

BUTTONS: Lost the jelly. Where is it, kids?

(The jelly slides across the stage (FSQ.16), wobbling. BUTTONS trying to catch it. The SISTERS collide. BUTTONS goes after it and returns carrying it, as the SISTERS get up. He wobbles backwards and forwards, trips and falls with his face in the jelly.)

GERTRUDE: Ooo look – a jelly baby!

GLADYS: Herh herh herh! He's been gunged!

BUTTONS: Come here, you . . . Just wait 'til I get my hands on you!
                (He chases them off.)

(LXQ.46; FSQ.16A)

(Music: A Waltz. FOOTMEN remove the tables and chairs as the PRINCE and CINDERELLA dance on, surrounded by LORDS and LADIES.)

PRINCE: This has been the most wonderful evening of my life . . .

CINDERELLA: And the most wonderful evening of mine.

PRINCE: I could dance with you like this the whole night through . . .

CINDERELLA: Oh, yes . . .

(LXQ.47)

(The Clock begins to chime for the hour.)

CINDERELLA: But . . .

PRINCE: What is it?

CINDERELLA: I must go . . .

PRINCE: Go? You can't go now – not ever – not now that I've found
               you again . . .

CINDERELLA: I must! I must!

PRINCE: No . . . No . . . Please . . . Stay . . .

CINDERELLA: I can't . . . ! I mustn't . . . ! I really can't . . .

(LXQ.48)

               *(She breaks away and runs through the dancers and up the
               stairs. The PRINCE tries to follow her but is unable to get
               through the crush. CINDERELLA goes off to R.)*

PRINCE: Stop her. That girl . . . The Princess . . . Stop her . . . Don't
               let her leave the palace!

MAJORDOMO: Right away, your Highness . . . *(He rushes up the stairs and
               exits to L.)*

DANDINI: *(Rushing after her)* I'll stop her, your Highness . . .

               *(Midnight strikes. CINDERELLA (substitute) immediately
               re-appears in her ragged clothes, collides with DANDINI
               and dashes across the landing to exit L.)*

DANDINI: Out of my way! Who on earth was that?

MAJORDOMO: *(Re-appears at the top of the stairs)* There's no sign of the
               Princess, your Highness . . .

PRINCE: No sign of her?

MAJORDOMO: Nor of anything or anyone. Except a kitchen maid running
               off through the grounds . . .

DANDINI: *(Pointing to the slipper on the stairs)* But look . . . That
               must be her slipper . . .

PRINCE: Let me see. Yes. This is one of the crystal slippers she was
               wearing. Then I shall find her. If it takes the rest of my
               life, I shall find her . . . Here, Dandini, take the slipper –

guard it with your life – and issue a proclamation that I shall marry the girl whose foot that slipper fits . . .

DANDINI: But . . .

PRINCE: Do it.   Tomorrow we begin our search.   Tomorrow we try the slipper on the foot of every young girl in the Kingdom. For tonight, leave me. I am fit for no more company . . . I wish to be alone.

(They all bow and retire.)

(LXQ.49; FSQ.17)

Song: FAR IN THE BLUE *(PRINCE, FAIRY)*

PRINCE: *(Moving to DL)* IS THIS A DREAM?
A LOVE THAT MIGHT HAVE BEEN –
THE FERVENT WISH OF MY IMAGINATION –
A LOVELY HALUCINATION?
SURELY SHE DWELLS
IN PARADISE DIVINE.
UPON MY HEART SHE CASTS HER MAGIC SPELL.
WHERE DOES SHE DWELL?
WILL SHE BE MINE?

(LXQ.50; FSQ.18)

FAIRY: *(Appears DR)* THERE ARE MAGIC COUNTRIES –
REMOTE AND UNEXPLORED
WHERE LOVE CAN FIND THE WAY;
WORLDS OF SHEER ENCHANTMENT –
WHERE HEARTS WITH ONE ACCORD
ARE GLAD AND BLITHE AND GAY!

PRINCE: LET ME BUT GO THERE –
WHERE I MAY FIND HER –
MY ARMS ENTWINE HER.
TO HER, MY DEAREST LOVE I'LL GO
SO –

PRINCE &   FAR IN THE BLUE –
FAIRY: BEYOND THE EVENING STARS –
THERE LIES A LAND OF DREAMS WHERE LOVE CAN
FIND ME/THEE –
THE DULL WORLD LEFT BEHIND ME/THEE.
FAR IN THE BLUE, IN EV'RY DREAM I/YOU DREAM,

MY/YOUR HEART IS YOURS/HERS, BELOV'D,
SOMEWHERE SO FAR BEYOND THE BLUE!

(Blackout.) *(LXQ.51; FSQ.17A & 18A; FlyQ.10)*

(LXQ.52)

Scene Two

The forest – night. (Front Cloth)
Nearby, a wolf howls (SQ.8). CINDERELLA runs on in her ragged dress.

BUTTONS: *(Off)* Cinders . . . Cinders, wait for me . . . Don't forget the wolf . . . !

CINDERELLA: The wolf? Oh no . . . ! *(Calling.)* Buttons? Buttons, where are you?

(A WOLF lopes on, howling and snarling. CINDERELLA screams and runs off. The WOLF sees the audience and moves threateningly towards them, stops and takes off his head.)

BUTTONS: Hello, you tinkers. Caw, what a night that was. Nearly missed midnight, didn't she? I was out in the yard minding my own business – talking to the ponies – there's a bloomin' big flash – coach turns into a pumpkin and the horses start nibbling round asking for cheese. But, here, I borrowed this costume off the Master of the Royal Revels. I'm going to get my own back on them ugly sisters. They'll be coming this way soon on their way back to Hardup Hall and I'm going to give 'em the fright of their lives . . .

GLADYS: *(Off)* Will you come on, Gertrude?

BUTTONS: Look out, here they come . . . *(He hides as the BARON and the SISTERS enter.)*

(SQ.9)

GERTRUDE: Oooooooh . . . Boooo-hoooooo . . . Icka Gerty don't like it here . . . Icka Gerty's f-f-frightened of f-f-f-forests and f-f-furry, f-f-ferocious w-wild f-f-fings like w-w-wolves . . .

GLADYS: Will you shut up, you big baby. I wonder what time it is?

BARON: I'll find out.

GLADYS: *(Hitting him)* Don't be stupid! You're as bad as her! How can you find out the time? There aren't any clocks in the forest.

BARON: *(Sings loud and tuneless)* "I'll take you home again, Kathleen . . .
            To where your heart has ever been . . .
            When first the fields were fresh and . . .

VOICE: *(Off, furious)* Will you stop that racket? Don't you know it's three o'clock in the morning?

BARON: It's three o'clock in the morning . . .

GERTRUDE: Three o'clock in the morning and here we are . . .

GLADYS: Where?

GERTRUDE: That's the p-p-p-point. We don't know *where* we are. We're l-l-l-l-l . . .

            (GLADYS hits her.)

GERTRUDE: Lost. WAAAAAHHH!

GLADYS: Will you shut up?

BARON: Ooooh. You've got to admit it's a bit creepy here though. I feel frightened, too.

GLADYS: Don't be so stupid. There is nothing to be frightened of.

BARON: What about that big hairy thing with the long teeth and the big nose?

GLADYS: Kenneth Clarke doesn't live anywhere near here.

BARON: I don't mean him, Gladys. I mean . . . the *wolf!*

            (Dramatic chord.)

GLADYS: The . . . *wolf?*

            (Dramatic chord.)

GERTRUDE: WAAAAAHHHH!

BARON: Now stop that. *(To the Orchestra.)* And you stop it, too.
                But I do feel frightened. Maybe we should sing a song to
                keep our spirits up.

GERTRUDE: Oh yes? And what if the wolf creeps up on us while we're
                meandering in a murmuring mist of melody?

BARON: Well, I'll ask my friends to watch out for us . . .

GLADYS: You've got friends?

                *(They set up "He's behind you" routine with the
                AUDIENCE.)*

BARON: Altogether now – *(They sing.)* Ging-gang-goolie-goolie-
                goolie- goolie-gotcha
                Ging gang gool, ging gang gool
                Ging-gang-goolie-goolie-goolie-goolie-gotcha
                Ging gang gool, ging gang gool.
                Hey-la, hey-la-shey-la, hey-la-shey-la hey la ho! *(And so on
                – though they never get any further because, each time, the
                wolf appears and frightens off first GLADYS then
                GERTRUDE then the BARON.)*

                *(The Wolf (BUTTONS) starts to sing when another ("real")
                Wolf creeps on behind him. When he finally becomes
                aware of it, he takes off his wolf's head. The real Wolf
                screams and runs off.)*

                (Blackout.)   **(LXQ.53; FlyQ.11)**

(LXQ.54; FSQ.19)

                            Scene Three

Hardup Hall – Tradesman's Entrance. (Front Cloth)
*Enter the PRINCE, DANDINI and the MAJORDOMO. DANDINI and the
MAJORDOMO carry posters.*

                Song: THE CRYSTAL SLIPPER *(PRINCE, DANDINI,
                MAJORDOMO)*

PRINCE: THROUGH THE LAND –
                PROCLAIM AT MY COMMAND –
                THE MAID WHOSE FOOT WILL FIT INSIDE
                THAT SLIPPER IS MY BRIDE.
                NOW GO!
                LET EV'RYBODY KNOW –

AND FIND MY SWEETHEART OUT WHERE E'ER SHE
HIDES

DANDINI &   ALL UP AND DOWN
MAJORDOMO: THROUGH FIELD AND TOWN
               WE'VE SEARCHED UNTIL OUR FEET ARE DROPPING OFF.
               WE'VE TRUDGED UNTIL
               WE'RE FEELING ILL

DANDINI: I'VE SUCH A NASTY COUGH!

DANDINI &   BOTH EAST AND WEST
MAJORDOMO: WE'VE DONE OUR BEST
               TO FIND YOUR PRINCESS BUT IT'S ALL IN VAIN.
               THERE'S NO ONE WHO
               FITS IN THAT SHOE

MAJORDOMO: AND NOW IT LOOKS LIKE RAIN!

DANDINI &   WE SOLEMNLY SWEAR –
MAJORDOMO: THE GIRL ISN'T THERE!
               BOTH HIGH AND LOW
               WE'VE SEARCHED, YOU KNOW –
               WE'VE STRETCHED UP AND WE'VE STOOPED!

               PLEASE GIVE US A BREAK –
               FOR COMRADESHIP'S SAKE –
               WE'VE WALKED UNTIL WE'RE WEARY AND WE'VE
               PEEPED UNTIL WE'RE POOPED!

PRINCE: SOUTH AND NORTH –
               I ORDER YOU 'GO FORTH!'
               DON'T FAIL OR FALTER IN YOUR QUEST –

DANDINI &   IT'S CLEAR THAT HE'S DEPRESSED!
MAJORDOMO:

PRINCE: PROCLAIM –
               THOUGH NO-ONE KNOWS HER NAME –
               MY HEART IS BROKEN

DANDINI &   BUT WE NEED A REST!
MAJORDOMO:

PRINCE: DON'T GIVE UP! DON'T YOU DARE TO FAIL!
               DON'T DARE RETURN IF YOU CANNOT BRING HER
               BACK WITH YOU.
               FIND HER OUT OR YOU GO TO JAIL

DANDINI & WELL THANKS A BUNCH! YOU CAN KEEP YOUR
MAJORDOMO: ROTTEN CRYSTAL SHOE!

IT'S KNEELING DOWN AND GETTING UP
THEN LOOKING FOR THE NEXT ONE ON THE LIST!
THEN KNEELING DOWN AND GETTING UP AND
WOND'RING WHO WE'VE MISSED!
WHERE IS THAT GIRL? WE'RE IN A WHIRL
FROM IN AND OUT AND RUNNING ALL ABOUT.
WE KNOCK ON DOORS AND KNEEL ON FLOORS
WE'RE GOING ROUND THE TWIST!

(Blackout.)   *(LXQ.55; FSQ.19A; FlyQ.12)*

(LXQ.56; FSQ.20)

Scene Four

The Kitchen of Hardup Hall.

Song: LOVE IS A SONG *(CINDERELLA)*

CINDERELLA: I HAD NOTHING BUT MY DREAMING –
ONLY LONELY, WISTFUL SONGS TO SING.
NOW I'VE RICHES – BRIGHT AND GLEAMING.
NOW I KNOW THE JOY THAT LOVE CAN BRING.

LOVE IS A SONG THAT NEVER ENDS,
LIFE MAY BE SWIFT AND FLEETING.
HOPE MAY DIE YET LOVE'S BEAUTIFUL MUSIC
COMES EACH DAY LIKE THE DAWN.
LOVE IS A SONG THAT NEVER ENDS;
ONE SIMPLE THEME REPEATING,
LIKE THE VOICE OF A HEAVENLY CHOIR,
LOVE'S SWEET MUSIC FLOWS ON.

(LXQ.57; FSQ.20A)

(The UGLY SISTERS enter in evil mode with chains and handcuffs.)

GERTRUDE: I don't know what *you've* got to sing about.

GLADYS: She can sing all she likes in the cellar!

GERTRUDE: Yeh. Nobody'll hear her . . .

CINDERELLA: Oh no. Please! Not the cellar!

GLADYS: Of course you're going in the cellar. We don't want you here when the Prince comes . . .

CINDERELLA: The Prince? Coming here?

GLADYS: Yeh. To see me.

GERTRUDE: Me.

GLADYS: And we don't want you showing us up. Grab her, Gert!

GERTRUDE: *(Seizing CINDERELLA)* Got her, Glad!

CINDERELLA: Oh no. Please! Don't lock me in the cellar . . .

GLADYS: *(Chaining her)* We *might* let you out again . . .

GERTRUDE: After one of us marries the Prince . . .

GLADYS: Unless we forget all about you and leave you to starve . . . !

(They exit, dragging CINDERELLA and cackling nastily.)

(LXQ.58)

(The BARON enters backwards, bowing, followed by DANDINI and the MAJORDOMO. The MAJORDOMO carries a cushion on which is the crystal slipper.)

DANDINI: I tell you, Baron, this won't do at all . . . The Prince will be here at any moment.

BARON: But why would the Prince want to come to see this rundown old ruin?

DANDINI: It isn't *you* he's coming to see. Surely you know that we bring this Crystal slipper and seek the maiden whose foot it fits. You have daughters, I believe.

BARON: Don't remind me.

DANDINI: Well, where are they?

BARON: I don't know where the nice one is but the two horrible ones were having hysterics in their room earlier and wouldn't come down.

DANDINI:	Kindly inform them that the Prince's representatives are here and wish to try it on . . .
BARON:	Oh well they might come down for that.
BUTTONS:	*(Rushes in)* Where is she? Where is she?
BARON:	Where's who?
BUTTONS:	Cinderella, of course. The Prince is here for her to try on the slipper and I can't find her anywhere . . .
BARON:	But don't be silly. Cinderella wasn't even *at* the ball.
BUTTONS:	Oh yes she was.
BARON:	Oh no she wasn't.
BUTTONS:	*(Leading the AUDIENCE)* Oh yes she was!
BARON:	*(To the AUDIENCE)* Was she?
AUDIENCE:	Yes.
BARON:	Well, I'm gobsmacked! But how? I mean where did she get a dress? And a carriage?
BUTTONS:	*(To the AUDIENCE)* SSSHHH! Our secret. *(To the BARON, shaking him.)* But I can't find her . . . Where is she? What have you done with Cinderella?
DANDINI:	This . . . Cinderella. Is she one of your daughters?
BUTTONS:	*(Looking under the table)* She's the only one . . . Cinders?
DANDINI:	*(Consulting his parchment)* But all I have down here is "Miss Gladys" and "Miss Gertrude".
BARON:	Oh them! I'll call them. *(Calling at the door.)* Gladys!
GLADYS:	*(Off)* Go away!
BARON:	Gertrude?
GERTRUDE:	*(Off)* Get lost!
	(The PRINCE enters briskly.)

PRINCE: Come on, Dandini, the horses are getting restless. What's the hold up?

DANDINI: A slight case of disappearing daughters, your Highness. One of the daughters is missing . . .

BUTTONS: *(Looking in cupboards, up the chimney, etc)* I'll find her, I tell you . . . Cinders . . . ?

DANDINI: The other two are changing.

PRINCE: Changing?

BUTTONS: Into vampire bats . . . I'll find her – I'll find her . . . *(To the AUDIENCE.)* Does anybody know where Cinderella is? *(Taking suggestions.)* Gone to see David Mellor? Gone to see the flower seller? Gone to have her hair dyed yeller? I'd better hurry up then. *(He runs off.)*

PRINCE: But these other two . . . Where are they?

GERTRUDE: *(Appears in the doorway – nauseous coyness)* Here I is, your Highness. Here is little me!

               (She is pushed and rocketed across the room as GLADYS enters.)

GLADYS: Pay no attention to her, your Highness. *I* is the one with the tiny tootsies what'll fit into a thimble . . .

DANDINI: Very well. Which of you is to try first?

GLADYS: Me!

GERTRUDE: Me!

DANDINI: Alphabetical order . . .

GERTRUDE: Then it's me cos "ert" comes before "ladys".

GLADYS: Wast of time. She takes a size twenty-seven in Doc Martins.

GERTRUDE: *You* can't talk. Her feet are so big they use them to stamp out forest fires. *(She sits on the stool.)*

PRINCE: But *she* isn't the one I danced with.

DANDINI: All the same . . . your proclamation says "*every* girl".

MAJORDOMO: *(Rudely)* Come on then, face-ache. Give us your foot.

GERTRUDE: You'll get it in your gob in a minute . . . I mean oh la, sir, fie, sir – fiddlededee – I've been meaning to cut my toenails since 1983.

DANDINI: Try the slipper, Majordomo.

GERTRUDE: *(Triumphant)* It fits! It fits! A perfect fit!

DANDINI: Get up and walk about a bit.

GERTRUDE: I'm rather weary just this minute . . .

DANDINI: Well?

MAJORDOMO: She's only got her big toe in it.

GLADYS: *(Knocking GERTRUDE off the stool)* You flipping fibber! You flibberteygibbet! Now . . . *(Sitting.)* to try on *my* slipper . . .

DANDINI: But I didn't dance with her *either* – and she *certainly* wasn't the girl in the woods.

GLADYS: You'll see, your Highness. I only looks like this in the morning. As the day goes on – I warm up. *(Sticking out a foot.)* Course I've got very musical feet . . .

GERTRUDE: Yeh. Both flat.

(The MAJORDOMO fits the slipper.)

GLADYS: Oooh hoo hoo . . . I'm so ticklish . . .

MAJORDOMO: *(Amazed)* It fits . . .

DANDINI: What?

PRINCE: I don't believe it . . .

MAJORDOMO: It's a perfect fit . . .

PRINCE: This can't be true . . .

DANDINI: *(Inspecting)* But I'm afraid it is, sire . . .

PRINCE: *(Appalled)* But I can't marry . . . *that!*

DANDINI: You gave your word, your Highness.

GLADYS: Yes! I know my rights. You issued a proclamation to the whole kingdom . . .

DANDINI: You *have* to marry her . . .

GLADYS: Yes, your Highchair – or may I call you Hubby . . . ? 'Twas I what was the belle of the ball and now I shall be the Princess Gladys. You may grovel, Gertrude. If you kneel and kiss my foot, I may get you off with one of the footmen . . . Foot-men – get it? Hee hee hee!

(GERTRUDE kneels and kisses her foot. BUTTONS enters.)

BUTTONS: I still can't find Cinderella.

GLADYS: Cinderella? I *might* let her be my ladies maid. And you, you silly little man. Kneel and kiss my foot. You heard me. Kneel.

(BUTTONS kneels and takes hold of her foot as if to kiss it.)

PRINCE: *(In shock)* I must go back to the palace and lie down!

GLADYS: And I shall come with you, your Highness, I shall ride in your carriage and chuck pebbles at the peasants . . .

PRINCE: *(Heading for the door)* I'M *OFF* . . . !

GLADYS: No wait for me, my darling – my hubby-wubby . . . wait for your little princess . . . *(She hops after him, leaving the display leg behind with BUTTONS. Everybody looks at the leg while she rattles on.)* I shall want a few changes made at that palace, of course. I mean, the decor – not an Oasis poster in sight – and I shall want all the furniture re-covered in pink fur fabric and . . . and . . . *(She sees the leg and bursts into tears.)* WAAAAAHHHHHH!

GERTRUDE: *(Beating her)* You rotten cheat!

PRINCE: Come on, Dandini, I'm off!

BUTTONS: But Cinderella must try the slipper on . . .

DANDINI: Too late! We're off!

*(There is a Flash **(PyroQ.6; LXQ.59; FSQ.21)** and the FAIRY GODMOTHER appears DR.)*

FAIRY: Hold!

PRINCE: Pardon?

FAIRY: Stay, Prince Charming, for in all this land.
The one you love is close at hand.

PRINCE: But . . . Who are you?

FAIRY: That need not concern you now.   Cinderella must try on the slipper.

BUTTONS: But nobody knows where Cinderella is.

FAIRY: You're wrong, Buttons. Gladys and Gertrude know.

GLADYS: We don't.

GERTRUDE: It's a lie.

FAIRY: *(Sternly)* What have you done with Cinderella?

GERTRUDE: Locked her away, didn't us?

GLADYS: *(Spitefully)* Yes. Yes we have.

GERTRUDE: *(Spitefully)* Somewhere where *you'll* never find her.

BOTH: Where *nobody* will ever find her!

GLADYS: Where she'll *starve* and *rot* to her dying day . . .

GERTRUDE: Where *nobody* will know where she is . . .

GLADYS: Nor hear her cries . . . nor . . .

FAIRY: *(To the AUDIENCE)* Does anyone know where they've imprisoned Cinderella?

AUDIENCE: THE CELLAR.

FAIRY: *(Chanting)* May all the powers of goodness and grace
Bring Cinderella to this place –
From where she lies in fright and fear –
I command you now! Let her . . . appear!

(Music. A Flash C. **(PyroQ.7; LXQ.60; FSQ.22)** *A column of coloured smoke and CINDERELLA, in chains, rises up through the floor.)*

BUTTONS: Cinders . . . You're safe . . . But in chains . . .

(The FAIRY waves her wand and the chains fall to the floor. CINDERELLA steps forward.)

PRINCE: It's you! It's her, Dandini . . . the girl I met in the woods . . . and the Princess who danced with me at the ball . . . I've found you at last and I shall never let you go again. This is the girl I shall marry . . . if she'll say yes . . .

DANDINI: But, Highness, you cannot marry her.

PRINCE: What?

DANDINI: Not unless the slipper fits.

BUTTONS: *(Leading her to the chair)* Here, Cinders, try the slipper . . .

(She sits. The PRINCE kneels and fits the slipper onto her foot.)

PRINCE: It fits!

BUTTONS: It fits!

BARON/
DANDINI/   It fits!
MAJORDOMO:

(LXQ.61; FSQs.21A & 22A)

GERTRUDE: I'm *having* a fit.

BARON: *(Sternly)* You two!

BUTTONS: You'd better watch out now . . . Chaining a princess up in a cellar . . .

BARON: That's high treason!

BUTTONS:	You'll have your heads chopped off!
GLADYS:	*(Grovelling)* Oh, darling little Cinders . . .
GERTRUDE:	*(Grovelling)* Lovely beautiful wonderful Cinders . . .
GLADYS:	Can you ever forgive us?
BUTTONS:	Forgive *you*? Never!
CINDERELLA:	Of course I can.
BUTTONS:	But they've bullied and beaten you all these years!
BARON:	They've chivvied and cheated and had you in tears!
BUTTONS:	They've shouted and shoved you and . . .
CINDERELLA:	I know – poor dears . . .
BUTTONS & BARON:	Poor dears?
CINDERELLA:	Oh Buttons, how could I be so happy and not forgive them?
BUTTONS:	*(Going to embrace her)* Oh, Cinders, you're so . . .
PRINCE:	*(Taking her hand and leading her away from BUTTONS)* Come, Cinderella, my carriage awaits To carry you off in royal state – *(BUTTONS turns away sadly.)* Away to my palace on yonder hill My kingdom is yours if you'll say: "I will".
CINDERELLA:	Of course I . . . oh but . . . wait a moment . . . Buttons?
BUTTONS:	Yes, Cinders?
CINDERELLA:	The Prince has asked me to marry him, but . . .
BUTTONS:	But?
CINDERELLA:	You've been so good to me all these years – since I was a little girl – my best friend – you've done all you could to make me happy . . .
BUTTONS:	All I ever wanted was to make you happy, Cinders . . .

CINDERELLA: But how can I be truly happy . . . if I go away from you?

BUTTONS: You *must* go, Cinders. Your *true* happiness lies with the Prince. Go with him. And may you both be happy all your days.

CINDERELLA: Oh, Buttons, I shall miss you . . .

PRINCE: But Buttons shall come with us. There's plenty of room at the Palace . . .

SISTERS: And us?

PRINCE: There isn't *that* much room. But come now. Your answer?
Will you marry me and be my bride?
And rule the Kingdom at my side?
Be my Princess – and my Queen one day?

CINDERELLA: What can I say but "yes?"

ALL: Hooray!

(Music, bells.)

FAIRY: Now all the bells throughout the Nation
Ring out a joyful proclamation.
May all be joy and mirth and laughter
And may Cinderella and her Prince be . . . happy ever after!

(LXQ.62; FSQ.23)

Song: SEARCHING FOR LOVE (Reprise) *(FULL COMPANY)*

(During which, the UGLIES don aprons, BUTTONS gives them buckets and they begin to scrub the floor.)

ALL: THEY WERE SEARCHING FOR LOVE;
FOR THIS MOMENT OF BLISS;
IT WAS FORETOLD ABOVE
THAT IT WOULD END LIKE THIS

GLADYS & NOW WE'RE RUB-A-DUB DUBBERS –
GERTRUDE: JUST A PAIR OF OLD SCRUBBERS

ALL: WHILE OUR PRINCE AND PRINCESS
HAVE FOUND TRUE HAPPINESS!

(Blackout.)   **(LXQ.63;   FSQ.23A;   FlyQ13)**

(LXQ.64;   FSQ.24)

Scene Five

A Country Lane.

BUTTONS and Songsheet. Announcements, parties, birthdays, etc.

> TWINKLE, TWINKLE, LITTLE STAR –
> HOW I WONDER WHAT YOU ARE.
> UP ABOVE THE WORLD SO HIGH –
> LIKE A DIAMOND IN THE SKY.
> TWINKLE, TWINKLE, LITTLE STAR –
> HOW I WONDER WHAT YOU ARE.

(LXQ.65;   FlyQ.14;   FSQ.24A)

Scene Six

The Ballroom of the Royal Palace.

Walkdown.

FINALE *(FULL COMPANY)*

ALL:　　　　　　WHATEVER
　　　　　　　　FORTUNE MAY HAVE BEEN SENDING
　　　　　　　　WE NEVER
　　　　　　　　DOUBTED THIS HAPPY ENDING;
　　　　　　　　WE KNEW IT, DIDN'T YOU?
　　　　　　　　A REWARD FOR LOVE THAT'S TRUE.
　　　　　　　　PROCLAIM IT!
　　　　　　　　AND LET NO-ONE DOUBT IT –
　　　　　　　　A SHAME IT
　　　　　　　　WOULD BE TO BE WITHOUT IT
　　　　　　　　FOR LOVE IS ALL,
　　　　　　　　AS YOU MAY RECALL,
　　　　　　　　WHEN THE CURTAIN'S DUE!

BUTTONS:　　　GERT AND GLADYS
　　　　　　　　ARE STILL A PAIR OF BADDIES

GLADYS &　　　IT'S NOT OUR FAULT
GERTRUDE:　　WE'RE JUST MISUNDERSTOOD
　　　　　　　　AND WE BOTH VOW

WE'LL BE NICE NOW!

BUTTONS: DO YOU THINK THAT YOU COULD?

GLADYS &   WELL, WE KNOW THAT WE SHOULD!
GERTRUDE:

ALL: HOORAY! THEY'LL/WE'LL BE GOOD!
AND NOW WE
WISH YOU WARM SEASON'S GREETINGS
AND HOW WE
HAVE ENJOYED THIS BRIEF MEETING
BUT NOW IT'S TIME
FOR THIS PANTOMIME
TO SAY "GOODBYE".

(Curtain.)   *(LXQ.66; FSQ.24B)*

OPTIONAL "SLOSH" SCENE

The following is a section which can be added – if you want it. It's very messy and adds to the overall running time but the kids (of all ages) love it. It fits in following the Trio in Act Two, Scene Three:

PRINCE: Here. Since you've tried everyone who was on the Palace mailing list – paste up this proclamation for the general public. Remember – there's a reward. *(He goes.)*

DANDINI: A reward!

MAJORDOMO: Or go to jail. Poor Prince – not like him to be nasty. He's proper put out.

DANDINI: Yes. We must do all we can to help him. Trouble is, we haven't any paste. However are we going to stick up this poster?

GERTRUDE: *(Off)* I want the blue with begonias . . .

GLADYS: *(Off)* And I want the pink with petunias . . .

GERTRUDE: Begonias . . . !

GLADYS: Petunias . . . !

(The UGLY SISTERS enter in overalls and bowler hats, hitting each other with rolls of wallpaper.)

DANDINI: Ah . . . er . . . ladies?

BOTH: Oh it's you!

GLADYS: What you want here?

DANDINI: I am on an errand for the Prince.

GLADYS: Oh, the Prince!

GERTRUDE: We don't care about the Prince no more!

GLADYS: 'Cos he don't care about us!

GERTRUDE: I suppose he's marrying that flibberteygibbet in the fancy frock.

DANDINI: No. Search as we may, she cannot be found . . .

BOTH: Oooooh . . . !

GERTRUDE: You mean he's still available?

GLADYS: Still up for grabs?

DANDINI: He has sworn that he will marry any girl in the kingdom . . .

GLADYS: Course I'm not just *any* girl . . .

DANDINI: Whose foot will fit the crystal slipper . . .

GLADYS: So there's still a chance . . .

DANDINI: That is my errand. I need to post up this proclamation for the Prince to help him find his own true love.

BOTH: Ooooh!

GLADYS: Well, we're your girls for sticking things up, young sir.

GERTRUDE: Yes. It does just so happen that we was on our way to wallpaper our boudoir in blue with begonias . . .

GLADYS: In pink with petunias . . .

GERTRUDE: Which is why we is all got up like this, see – ready for a right good pasting.

DANDINI: Very well. Here. I shall leave it in your hands. Don't let me down now.

GERTRUDE: You can count on us.

GLADYS: You lick it – we stick it.

GERTRUDE: Stick it up, stick it down, stick it all around the village.

DANDINI: *(Doubtfully)* Yes . . . Come on, Majordomo. We'll leave it to the ladies . . . *(They exit.)*

GLADYS: Now we shall need some icky sticky goo.

GERTRUDE: Icky sticky goo for me and you.

BOTH:	BUTTONS!
BUTTONS:	*(Enters pushing a trolley containing buckets of slosh and brushes with a ladder on top)* You called?
GLADYS:	Well that's handy.
GERTRUDE:	Ah Buttons, I see you've brought the Tesco trolley . . .
BUTTONS:	*(Spreading tarpaulin, to AUDIENCE)* Oh yes we are . . . !
GLADYS:	*(Putting the ladder up)* You can go away now. We is doing this for the Prince. We don't need you, you *little* man.
BUTTONS:	Oh yes you do.
GERTRUDE:	Oh no we don't.
BUTTONS:	Oh yes you do.
BOTH:	Oh shut up.
	(GERTRUDE takes a bucket of slosh. She pours it into another bucket which GLADYS is holding – it has no bottom – it goes all over her.)
GLADYS:	Oh now look what you've done. Look, I'll get another bucket and you get up the ladder.
	(GERTRUDE goes up the ladder while GLADYS holds a bucket of slosh on top of her head. GERTRUDE dips her brush and flicks it all over GLADYS. GLADYS is furious.)
GLADYS:	No no no. I'll do it.
	(They swop places and repeat the biz – all over GERTRUDE. BUTTONS falls about.)
GERTRUDE:	Here you! Stop that and take this.
	(BUTTONS takes the bucket from GERTRUDE and puts it down at the foot of the ladder. GLADYS comes down and puts her foot in the bucket.)
GLADYS:	Right, that's it.

(GLADYS picks up bucket with no bottom – looks through at audience. She gives it to BUTTONS to hold. She turns to pick up full bucket of slosh. BUTTONS turns to give the hole bucket to GERTRUDE and picks up the third bucket (which has a wee-wee hole). GLADYS turns to fill up the bucket BUTTONS is holding, sniggering the while. BUTTONS keep his finger over the hole while it is filled up. He climbs ladder while GERTRUDE and GLADYS look puzzled.)

BUTTONS: Get the brush, please . . .

(He does flicking biz. They approach holding hole bucket. BUTTONS lets wee-wee hole go. They go "aah" and hold up hole bucket – over both of them while they get soaked.)

GERTRUDE: *(Gives GLADYS the poster to hold up)* Now get that and stick it up you stupid trollop.

(GLADYS takes it and GERTRUDE turns to load the brush. BUTTONS taps GLADYS on shoulder. She turns. GERTRUDE turns round and paints GLADYS'S back. BUTTONS takes the poster from GLADYS.)

GERTRUDE: Not that way, you stupid woman. Turn round.

(GLADYS turns. GERTRUDE loads the brush and paints her front. They plot to do the same to BUTTONS. BUTTONS holds up the poster and they paste it violently but it keeps him clean. After a series of manouvres, he ducks out of the way and the girls end up painting each other.)

BUTTONS: You're supposed to paint it on the backside.

(They turn the poster round and paint other side. BUTTONS takes the poster up the ladder and destroys it by stepping on it all the way up. He is left with a tiny fragment which he sticks up.)

GLADYS: No, no, you stupid little man. Let us do it.

(They take the bowler hat off BUTTONS and GERTRUDE fills it up with slosh.)

GLADYS: Oh Buttons . . .

BUTTONS: Yes Gladys . . .

GLADYS: *(Leading him to GERTRUDE)* Just come here a moment . . .

GERTRUDE: *(to the AUDIENCE)* Shall I?

AUDIENCE: Yes.

> *(She turns to put the bowler on BUTTONS' head.*
> *BUTTONS ducks out of the way and it goes onto GLADYS'S*
> *head. BUTTONS pulls it down and a jet of slosh spurts*
> *into the air.)*

> *(Blackout.)*

There are various kinds of patent "Slosh" on the market these days but we've never found anything to beat the old fashioned mixture which can be made thicker or thinner according to the demands of the routine. This is made by grating shaving soap into a bucket of cold water and whisking it up with the biggest food whisk you can find until it's the right consistency for the effect. It can be coloured using food colouring.

Just as anything to do with sausages owes its origins to Joey Grimaldi, so our slosh routines are contrived in loving memory of Charlie Cairolli who turned "slosh" into an art form and who delighted so many countless millions at Blackpool Tower Circus and on television.

Props Plot

ACT ONE

Prologue – BEFORE "CAMEO" CLOTH.

Wand for FAIRY GODMOTHER.
Huge prop Pie – for STEPMOTHER.
Broom, Mop, Bucket, Feather Duster – all for CINDERELLA.

Scene One – THE VILLAGE GREEN. OUTSIDE HARDUP HALL.

Sheaf of Bills for BARON HARDUP.
Duster, Bucket and Mop for CINDERELLA.
Tricycle or Bicycle for BUTTONS – dressed up as a travelling
    toyshop, festooned with dolls, toys and teddy bears,
    windmills, streamers, flags, bells, etc.
Tennis racquet clipped onto above.
Basket or bag of Marshmallows on above.

Scene Two – A STATEROOM IN THE ROYAL PALACE. (FRONT CLOTH)

Hunting Horn for DANDINI.
Royal Hat, Sash, Sword, Garter Star for the PRINCE (must be easily
    removed and put onto DANDINI).

Scene Three – THE FOREST.

Riding Crops for BARON, MAJORDOMO, HUNSTMEN and
    WOMEN.
Basket of twigs for CINDERELLA.
Twigs set here and there for gathering.
FROG (glove puppet) – operated from behind a fallen log.
Walking Stick for FAIRY GODMOTHER.

The Hobbyhorses: (For BUTTONS, the BARON, GLADYS and
    GERTRUDE) These should look rather pretty and are built
    on the lines of a crinoline frame with a head and tail on.
    They are supported on shoulder straps, have "jousting"
    skirts which come to the floor and silly little legs attached
    to the saddles, matching what the actor is wearing. They
    are controlled by the reins.

Haversack for BUTTONS containing Glasses (plastic).

Haversack for the BARON containing Bottle of Wine.

Scene Five – THE INTERIOR OF BUTTONS' TOYSHOP.

There are toys and teddy bears hanging and on shelves everywhere. A large chest of drawers stands C. The bottom drawer pulls out to be BUTTONS' bed. There is a workbench to one side. This has a vice and various oversize tools – including a big (rubber or foam) hammer and a gigantic monkey wrench (also rubber or foam). Large (Dancers) Dolls – Soldiers, Ballerinas, Dutchdolls, a Fairy, Woodentop Dolls, etc, lean in boxes against the walls or are sprawled about the floor.

> Teddy's body in the Vice.
> Curly Blonde Doll's head (to be – apparently – nailed onto the
>   Teddy's body).
> Torn Teddy Bear for GERTRUDE.
> Handbell for the MAJORDOMO.
> Parchment List of Guests for MAJORDOMO.
> Tickets for MAJORDOMO – one for GLADYS, one for GERTRUDE.
> Large, colourful Ball – in the top drawer of the Chest (to open and
>   roll out by magic).

The Dress is assembled onto the dummy before our very eyes with the Dolls bringing (apparently) raw fabric which can be velcroed (apparently stitched) into the finished garment.

> Bugle for TOY SOLDIER.
> Wand for FAIRY DOLL.
> Toy Crocodile to use as Scissors.
> Large Needle.
> Balls of Thread.

Scene Seven – THE UGLY SISTERS' BOUDOIR.

Dressing-tables either side, stool for each. A door UC.

> Huge Nailfile for GLADYS.
> Basket of awful assorted knickers – among which is a huge pair of
>   bloomers with a large hole right through – for GERTRUDE.
> Awful lace-up Corsets for BOTH.
> Very large Lipstick for GERTRUDE (practical but soft – sponge end?
>   She hits GLADYS in the mouth with it).
> Huge can of cold cream for GERTRUDE.
> Huge cannister of powder labelled VIM – for GERTRUDE.
> Gigantic Cotton Bud for GLADYS.
> Huge Brillo Pad for GERTRUDE.
> Huge Flit Spray labelled LE HARPIC – for GERTRUDE.
> Pair of pointed Road Cones – for GLADYS – which velcro onto her

corset to make a "Madonna" bra.
Two huge plastic Flowers for GLADYS.
Necklace of Carrots for GLADYS.
Telephone Book (already cut in half and velcroed) for BUTTONS to
    tear.

Buttons' Permanent Prinking and Perming Appliance: This is a machine with
as many dials, knobs, switches, guages, coils of wire, valves, taps, etc, as
possible. It hinges open so that the SISTERS can put their heads in and
then be trapped. (They need to get their hands in also to carry out the
makeup and wig change.) There is a funnel on top of the machine to take
the shampoo. Ideally, smoke can be pumped into it – and pour out of it.

Stripey toy rabbit – inside the machine.
Huge Bottle of Shampoo (WASH'N'GO).
Huge Bottle of Shampoo (GO 'N' WASH).
Soda Syphon (practical) on Dressing Table.

Scene Eight – THE KITCHEN OF HARDUP HALL.

Fireplace UC. Table LC. Two Stools before the Fire.

Invitation – for BUTTONS.
The "Dress" – for BUTTONS.
Broom by the Fireplace.
Tablecloth on Table (with velcro for CINDERELLA to wear as a
    Skirt).
Spatula in the saucepan (for Fan).
Big pair of Wellingtons.
String of Onions (Necklace).
Bowl of Cherries (pair as Ear-rings).
Hearthrug (with velcro – to be her Cape).
Cake Frill on Table (to be her Crown).
Two Copper Coalscuttles (for BUTTONS to wear as Boots).
Saucepan (for BUTTONS to wear as a Helmet).
Apron (for BUTTONS' Cape).
A pair of Oven Gloves.

"Repaired" Invitation from the Fire: A track of fishing line is rigged from
inside the fireplace to a corner of the mantelpiece. A small bulldog clip
travels on this (pulled by a second line), holding the Invitation for
BUTTONS to "catch".

Pumpkin.
Six Mice.
Lizard.
Two White Rats (could come up on the trap if there is one –
    otherwise pushed on, covered by PyroQ.3 and LXQ.36).

The Transformation: This is where the periaktoi come into their own but there are lots of other ways of doing this and any transformation is going to include things flying, things turning, things tracking on and off, etc. Whichever way, it reveals the Fairy Coach in the Fairy Forest drawn by either real (or Dancer) ponies.

ACT TWO

Scene One – THE BALLROOM OF THE PALACE.

Off Stage: Two round tables with tablecloths.
     Two dining chairs.
     Handbell on each table.
     Serviette on each table.
     Cutlery and condiments on each table.
     Bowl of soup (with small figure "swimming" in it).
     Plover's-egg pizza (two eggs to eat and one rubber one).
     Tea Trolley.
     Tureen of Spaghetti (with length of white elastic) – on the
       trolley.
     Huge red (very wobbly) jelly on platter.

   Waiter's pad and pencil for BUTTONS.
   Tiny fishing rod (with magnet to catch the swimmer) for BUTTONS.
   Pair of scissors for BUTTONS.

Scene Three – HARDUP HALL. TRADESMAN'S ENTRANCE. (FRONT CLOTH)

   Posters for DANDINI and the MAJORDOMO.

Scene Four – THE KITCHEN OF HARDUP HALL.

   Chains (plastic) for the SISTERS to chain up CINDERELLA.
   The Crystal Slipper – on a cushion – offstage.
   False leg (stocking display type) for GLADYS – offstage.

Scene Five – A COUNTRY LANE. (FRONT CLOTH)

   Songsheet.

Lighting Plot

ACT ONE

Cue	Detail
1	**(PyroQ.1)** Pick up FAIRY GODMOTHER DR.
2	Lights up behind the Cameo Cloth (*or Gauze*).
3	Fade the Cameo lighting.
4	(*Gauze flies out*) Bright Winter's day for OPENING NUMBER.
5	Brighten for BUTTONS' entrance.
6	Very colourful for BUTTONS' song with CHORUS.
7	Snap B.O.
8	Bright "Acting Light" – The Palace (*Front Cloth*).
9	Reduced and colourful for Prince/Dandini Duet.
10	Snap B.O.
11	The Woods – bright Winter's day – HUNTING CHORUS.
12	Romantic – CINDERELLA'S entrance.
13	**(PyroQ.2)** Lights down/up – to allow FAIRY to disappear.
14	*Very* Romantic – CINDERELLA/PRINCE meet.
15	State of LXQ.12.
16	State of LXQ.11.
17	State of LXQ.12.
18	State of LXQ.14.
19	State of LXQ.12.
20	State of LXQ.11.
21	Cross Fade to Front Cloth as it flies in – very bright day.
22	Swift Cross Fade to tight "leafy" Romantic areas DR and DL for Duet.
23	Fade B.O.
24	BUTTONS' Toyshop – evening (candle) but bright enough for comedy.
25	BUTTONS blows out the candle – moonlight – magical.
26	Cross Fade to Front Cloth – Night.
27	Snap B.O.
28	The Boudoir – bright.
29	Snap B.O.
30	The Kitchen – very romantic for CINDERELLA solo.
31	The Kitchen – "Acting Light" – evening.
32	Reduce to emphasise CINDERELLA lonely by the fire.
33	Romatic – a little magic – BUTTONS/CINDERELLA duet.

34	Return to State of LXQ.31.
35	Very magical – beginning of the spell.
36	**(Pyro Q.3)** Down/Up for RATS to appear.
37	**(Pyro Q.4)** Down/Up – CINDERELLA transformed – Ball Gown.
38	**(PyroQ.5)** TRANSFORMATION – to the Fairy Woodland – glittery, mysterious.
39	Brighten – the carriage and horses.
40	Build for end of Act One Finale.
41	Lose FOH as Curtain falls – leaving onstage tableau.

ACT TWO

42	The Palace – the Ball – very golden and glittering – Polka.
43	Bright for UGLIES' entrance.
44	Very beautiful and romantic for CINDERELLA entrance.
45	Brighten for comedy.
46	Return swiftly to state of LXQ.44.
47	Creep up light on the Clock, reduce area to PRINCE and CINDERELLA.
48	Very dramatic as CINDERELLA makes her escape.
49	Cross Fade to area DL for PRINCE.
50	Add area DR for FAIRY.
51	Fade B.O.
52	The Forest (*Front Cloth*) – night.
53	Snap B.O.
54	Bright day – Outside Hardup Hall – (*Front Cloth*).
55	Snap B.O.
56	The Kitchen – very romantic for CINDERELLA solo.
57	Very dramatic and sinister for chaining of CINDERELLA.
58	The same scene – but lift fairly swiftly to bright day.
59	**(PyroQ.6)** Down/Up – becomes magical as the FAIRY appears.
60	**(PyroQ.7)** Down to mysterious/very dramatic/sun bursting out as CINDERELLA appears and the chains fall to the ground.
61	Very bright for "It fits!" – happy ending.
62	Still bright but romantic for Song.
63	Snap B.O.
64	Front Cloth – very bright for SONGSHEET.
65	Swift Cross Fade as cloth flies out – to full up for Walkdown and Finale.
66	Fade FOH as Curtain Falls – leaving onstage tableau.

FOLLOW SPOT PLOT

ACT ONE

Cue	Effect – Stage R Spot	Effect – Stage L Spot
1	FAIRY DR.	FAIRY DR.
1A	Fade B.O. 5 secs.	Fade B.O. 5 secs.
2	CINDERELLA C.	CINDERELLA C.
2A	Fade B.O.	Fade B.O.
3	GLADYS – include CINDERS as poss.	GERTRUDE – include C as poss.
3A	Fade B.O.	Fade B.O.
4	BUTTONS.	BUTTONS.
4A	Snap B.O.	Snap B.O.
5	DANDINI.	PRINCE.
5A	Snap B.O.	Snap B.O.
6	MAJORDOMO.	BARON.
6A	Snap B.O.	Snap B.O.
7	CINDERELLA.	PRINCE.
7A	Fade B.O. 10 secs.	Fade B.O. 10 secs.
8	CINDERELLA.	PRINCE.
8A	Fade B.O. 5 secs.	Fade B.O. 5 secs.
9	CINDERELLA.	PRINCE.
9A	Fade B.O. 5 secs.	Fade B.O. 5 secs.
10	Pinspot BUTTONS.	Pinspot BUTTONS.
10A	Snap B.O.	Snap B.O.
11	CINDERELLA.	CINDERELLA.
11A	Fade B.O. 5 secs.	Fade B.O. 5 secs.
12	CINDERELLA.	BUTTONS.
12A	Fade B.O. 5 secs.	Fade B.O. 5 secs.
13		FAIRY.
14	CINDERELLA.	
13A & 14A	Fade to B.O. with CURTAIN.	

ACT TWO

15	CINDERELLA.	CINDERELLA.
15A	Fade B.O.	Fade B.O.
16	Pinspot on JELLY.	Pinspot on JELLY.
16A	Snap B.O.	Snap B.O.
17	PRINCE.	
18		FAIRY.
17A & 18A	Fade B.O. 5 secs.	
19	PRINCE.	DANDINI and MAJORDOMO.
19A	Snap B.O.	Snap B.O.
20	CINDERELLA.	CINDERELLA.
20A	Fade B.O. 5 secs.	Fade B.O. 5 secs.
21	FAIRY.	
22		CINDERELLA.
21A & 22A	Fade B.O. 5 secs	
23	CINDERELLA.	PRINCE.
23A	Snap B.O.	Snap B.O.
24	BUTTONS.	BUTTONS.
24A	Follow all CALLS.	Follow all CALLS.
24B	Fade B.O. with CURTAIN.	Fade B.O. with CURTAIN.

Sound Plot

Cue	Detail
1	Gaggle of giggling girls.
2	Wolf howls.
3	Bird song.
4	Bird song.
5	Bird song.
6	Series of machine noises – developing – slurping, clanking, grunting, whirring, etc.
7	Transformation – rushing wind – possible separate cue of joyful bells.
8	Wolf howls.
9	Owl hoots.

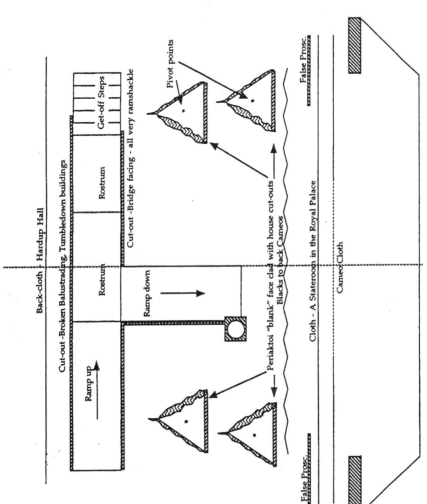

Back-cloth : Hardup Hall

Cut-out - Broken Balustrading, Tumbledown buildings

Cut-out - Bridge facing - all very ramshackle

Get-off Steps

Rostrum

Rostrum

Ramp up

Ramp down

Pivot points

Periaktoi "blank" face clad with house cut-outs
Blacks to back Cameos

Cloth - A Stateroom in the Royal Palace

False Prosc.

False Prosc.

Cameo Cloth

Act One: Prologue and Scenes 1 and 2

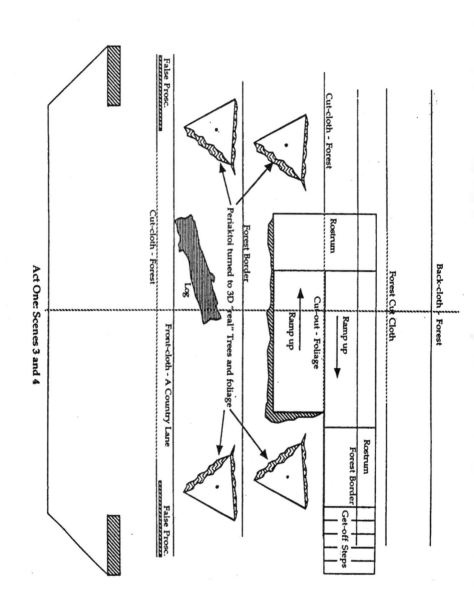

Act One: Scenes 3 and 4

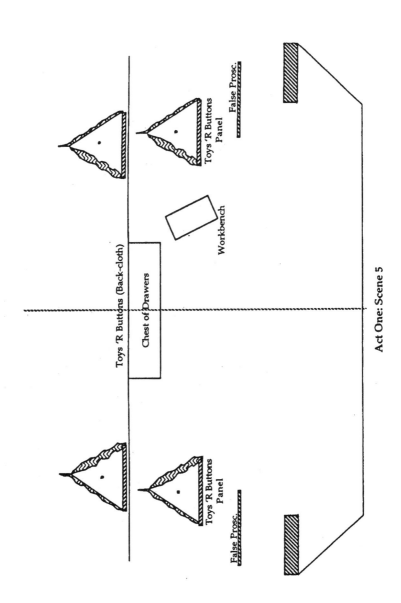

Act One: Scene 5

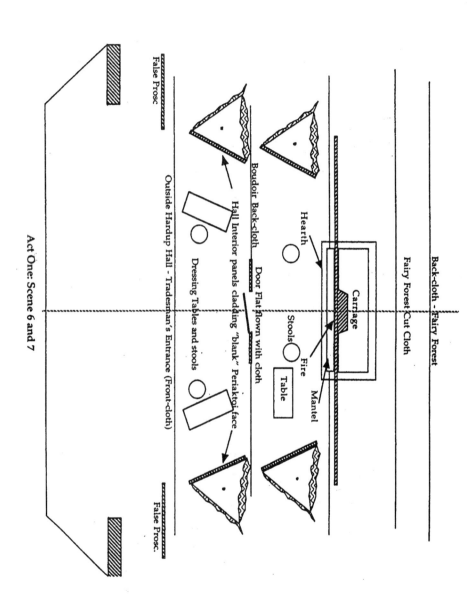

False Prosc

False Prosc.

Back-cloth - Fairy Forest

Fairy Forest Cut Cloth

Boudoir Back-cloth

Hall Interior panels cladding "blank" Periaktoi face

Door Flat flown with cloth

Hearth

Mantel

Fire

Stools

Table

Carriage

Dressing Tables and stools

Outside Hardup Hall - Tradesman's Entrance (Front-cloth)

Act One: Scene 6 and 7

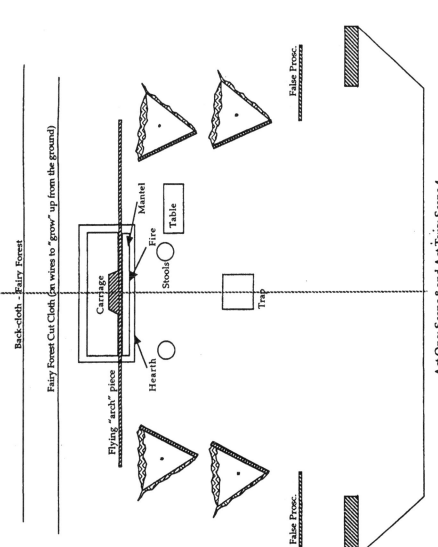

Back-cloth - Fairy Forest

Fairy Forest Cut Cloth (on wires to "grow" up from the ground)

Mantel

Table

Fire

Carriage

Stools

Flying "arch" piece

Hearth

Trap

False Prosc.

False Prosc.

Act One: Scene 8 and Act Two: Scene 4

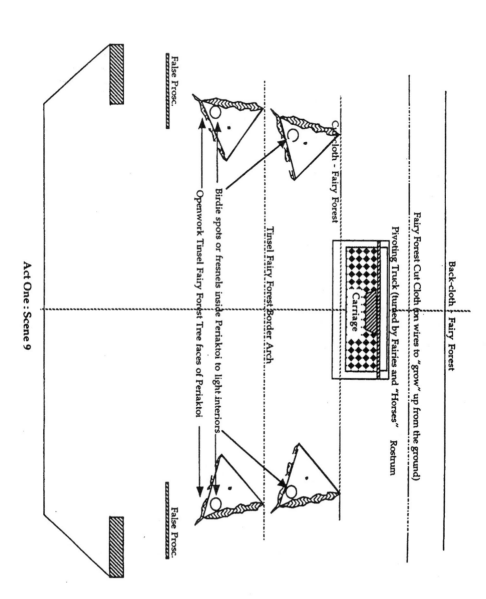

Act One : Scene 9

False Prosc.

Cloth - Fairy Forest

Birdie spots or fresnels inside Periaktoi to light interiors

Openwork Tinsel Fairy Forest Tree faces of Periaktoi

Tinsel Fairy Forest Border Arch

False Prosc.

Fairy Forest Cut Cloth (on wires to "grow" up from the ground)

Pivoting Truck (turned by Fairies and "Horses") Rostrum

Carriage

Back-cloth : Fairy Forest